Sylvan
Learning sm

At Sylvan, we believe reading is among life's most important skills, and we're glad you've chosen our resources to help your child build this crucial knowledge. A successful reader is ready for the world around him, and his imagination will be ready to flow to new heights; or, he can use these skills to do research and make the important connections necessary to achieve in school. With these skills, children will be successful in life as well as in school.

At Sylvan, reading instruction uses a step-by-step process with research-based and thought-provoking lessons. With success, students become more confident. With increasing confidence, students build even more success. That's why our Sylvan workbooks aren't like the others; we're laying out the roadmap for learning.

We're excited to partner with you to support the development of a confident, well-prepared independent learner!

The Sylvan Team

D1385162

Sylvan Learning Center.
Unleash your child's potential here.

No matter how big or small the academic challenge, every child has the ability to learn. But sometimes children need help making it happen. Sylvan believes every child has the potential to do great things. And we know better than anyone else how to tap into that academic potential so that a child's future really is full of possibilities. Sylvan Learning Center is the place where your child can build and master the learning skills needed to succeed and unlock the potential you know is there.

The proven, personalized approach of our in-center programs deliver unparalleled results that other supplemental education services simply can't match. Your child's achievements will be seen not only in test scores and report cards but outside the classroom as well. And when he starts achieving his full potential, everyone will know it. You will see a new level of confidence come through in everything he does and every interaction he has.

How can Sylvan's personalized in-center approach help your child unleash his potential?

- Starting with our exclusive Sylvan Skills Assessment®, we pinpoint your child's exact academic needs.

- Then we develop a customized learning plan designed to achieve your child's academic goals.

- Through our method of skill mastery, your child will not only learn and master every skill in his personalized plan, he will be truly motivated and inspired to achieve his full potential.

To get started, simply contact your local Sylvan Learning Center to set up an appointment. And to learn more about Sylvan and our innovative in-center programs, call 1-800-EDUCATE or visit www.SylvanLearning.com. *With over 750 locations in North America, there is a Sylvan Learning Center near you!*

5th Grade
Reading Comprehension
Success Workbook

Published in the United States by Random House, Inc., New York, and in Canada by Random House of Canada Limited, Toronto.

This book was previously published with the title *5th Grade Reading Comprehension Success* as a trade paperback by Sylvan Learning, Inc., an imprint of Penguin Random House LLC, in 2009.

www.sylvanlearning.com

Created by Smarterville Productions LLC
Cover and Interior Photos: Jonathan Pozniak
Cover and Interior Illustrations: Delfin Barral
Cover Design: Suzanne Lee

First Edition

ISBN: 978-0-375-43010-7

Library of Congress Cataloging-in-Publication Data available upon request.

This book is available at special discounts for bulk purchases for sales promotions or premiums. For more information, write to Special Markets/Premium Sales, 1745 Broadway, MD 6-2, New York, New York 10019 or e-mail specialmarkets@randomhouse.com.

PRINTED IN CHINA

10 9 8 7 6 5 4 3 2

Contents

Checking your answers is part of the learning.

Each section of the workbook begins with an easy-to-use Check It! strip.

1. Before beginning the activities, cut out the Check It! strip.

2. As you complete the activities on each page, check your answers.

3. If you find an error, you can correct it yourself.

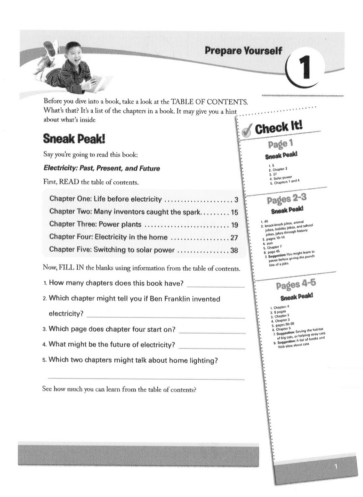

Before you dive into a book, take a look at the TABLE OF CONTENTS. What's that? It's a list of the chapters in a book. It may give you a hint about what's inside

Sneak Peak!

Say you're going to read this book:

Electricity: Past, Present, and Future

First, READ the table of contents.

Now, FILL IN the blanks using information from the table of contents.

1. How many chapters does this book have? _____

2. Which chapter might tell you if Ben Franklin invented

   electricity? _____

3. Which page does chapter four start on? _____

4. What might be the future of electricity? _____

5. Which two chapters might talk about home lighting?

   _____

See how much you can learn from the table of contents?

Pages 6-7

Sneak Peak!

1. plants, mammals, fish, coral reefs
2. at the bottom of the sea (or chapter 9)
3. chapter 1
4. chapters 10, 11, 13, 14, 16

Suggestions:

5. What creatures can live at the bottom of the sea?
6. How deep into the ocean can humans travel?
7. What is the effect of global warming on the Arctic Ocean?
8. How many oceans are there in the world?

Page 8

Sneak Peak!

Suggestions:

1. When was NASCAR started?
2. How is a stock car different from an Indy 500 car?
3. What happens during a stock car race?

Sneak Peak!

Say you're going to read this book:

First, READ the table of contents.

Now, FILL IN the blanks using information from the table of contents.

1. At least how many pages does this book have? _____

2. What kinds of jokes does it cover? _____

_____

_____

3. Which pages might have a joke about a duck? _____

4. What's another word for "a play on words"? _____

5. Which chapter might talk about the oldest joke ever told? _____

6. Which page has a list of all the jokes in the book? _____

7. What's one thing you might learn in chapter eight? _____

_____

Sneak Peak!

Say you're going to read this book:

First, READ the table of contents.

Now, FILL IN the blanks using information from the table of contents.

1. Which chapter might describe how cats catch mice? _____

2. How long is chapter seven? _____

3. Which chapter might tell you how many bones a tiger has? _____

4. Which chapter might tell you where leopards live? _____

5. Which pages might tell you about how to treat fleas on your cat? _____

6. Which chapter might cover cats' grooming habits? _____

7. What do you think chapter ten is about? _____

_____

8. What do you think you'll find on page 65? _____

_____

Sneak Peak!

Say you're going to read this book:

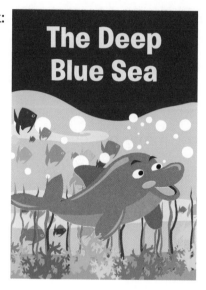

First, READ the table of contents.

Now, FILL IN the blanks using information from the table of contents.

1. What kinds of ocean life does this book cover? _____

   _____

2. Where is "the midnight zone" of the ocean? _____

   _____

3. Which chapter might list the names of the Earth's oceans? _____

4. Which chapters might deal with the effect of humans on the oceans?

   _____

Don't forget, the table of contents is just a clue to all the information in the book. WRITE four more questions that this book might answer that the table of contents can't.

5. _____

6. _____

7. _____

8. _____

Prepare Yourself

Sneak Peak!

Say you're going to read this book:

First, READ the table of contents.

WRITE three questions that this book might answer that the table of contents can't.

1. _____

2. _____

3. _____

 **Check It!**

Cut out the Check It! section on page 1, and see if you got the answers right.

The table of contents tells you what information is inside a book. But what about the information inside your head? The next step is to think about what you already know about a topic.

First, FILL IN the What Do I Already Know? section. After that, you'll be ready to read!

Topic: Burping

What Do I Already Know?

_____

_____

_____

What Did I Learn?

_____

_____

_____

Now, READ this article.

Excuse Me!

The air that we suck into our lungs contains important gases we couldn't live without. But sometimes we swallow those gases. Then our stomachs have to blast it out. The quickest way is through the mouth—Burrrrrpp! The *other* way can take 30 to 40 minutes. You may pass gas 15 times a day, passing about a quart of gas! Too bad you can't use it to fuel a car, huh?

Time to go back and FILL IN the What Did I Learn? section. CROSS OUT any facts in the first section you got wrong. See how this works?

✓ Check It!

Page 9

Suggestions:
Know:
1. Burping is caused by gas.
2. Some people can burp on purpose.
3. Drinking soda makes you burp.

Learned:
1. Air is filled with gas.
2. Burps move very fast.
3. Every day you pass about a quart of gas.

Pages 10-11

Before & After Questions
Suggestions:
Know:
1. Mount Rushmore is a giant carving of famous heads.
2. It's a big tourist attraction.
3. ~~One of the heads is Ben Franklin.~~

Learned:
1. The monument was built to be a tourist attraction.
2. Susan B. Anthony was proposed as an addition.
3. The monument has only been washed once.

Pages 12-13

Before & After Questions
Suggestions:
Know:
1. Monkeys live in jungles.
2. Monkeys eat bananas.
3. ~~Monkeys and apes are the same thing~~

Learned:
1. Monkeys are not apes.
2. Monkeys also eat insects.
3. NASA sent a monkey into outer space.

✓ Check It!

Pages 14-16

Before & After Questions

Suggestions:

Know:
1. China has the most people.
2. Chinese people celebrate their New Year at a different time than in Western culture.
3. ~~China is smaller than the United states.~~

Learned:
1. China is the most populous country and the third largest in size.
2. Paper, gunpowder, the compass, and printing were invented in China.
3. There are more Chinese restaurants in the United States than there are McDonald's restaurants.

Before & After Questions

FILL IN the What Do I Already Know? section.

Topic: Mount Rushmore

What Do I Already Know?

_____

_____

_____

_____

_____

_____

What Did I Learn?

_____

_____

_____

_____

_____

_____

_____

_____

_____

_____

Now, READ the article.

Heads of State

Every year, two million people visit Mount Rushmore in South Dakota. And that's a good thing because, from the very beginning, the giant sculpture was meant to be a tourist attraction. A historian named Doane Robinson had the idea in 1923 as a way to bring people to the beautiful Black Hills region of South Dakota.

It took fourteen years for sculptor Gutzon Borglum and 400 workers to sculpt the enormous 60-foot (18-meter) carvings of George Washington, Thomas Jefferson, Theodore Roosevelt, and Abraham Lincoln.

But no ladies were allowed. In 1937, Congress considered adding the head of Susan B. Anthony to the mountain, but the plan fell through. Also, the original plan was for the carvings to include the upper bodies of the presidents, but the money ran out before they could finish.

To take care of the monument, mountain climbers crawl all over the faces every year to find and seal cracks. The presidents have only washed their faces once—in 2005, using a high-pressure hot-water hose!

Did you learn anything? Go back and FILL IN the What Did I Learn? section.

Before & After Questions

FILL IN the What Do I Already Know? section.

Topic: Monkeys

What Do I Already Know?

_____
_____
_____
_____
_____
_____
_____

What Did I Learn?

_____
_____
_____
_____
_____
_____
_____
_____

Now, READ the article.

Monkey Business

There are so many kinds of monkeys! More than 200 kinds, to be exact. The smallest monkey is the Pygmy Marmoset, which is only five to six inches long. On the other hand, a big male Mandrill can be three feet tall and weigh 77 pounds. Some monkeys live in the trees, while others live in the dry grasslands called *savanna*.

All monkeys belong to the primate family, but not all primates are monkeys. Lemurs, apes, and humans are also primates. And guess what? Chimpanzees and gorillas aren't monkeys—they're apes. Although most people use the words *ape* and *monkey* to mean the same thing, zoologists know the difference.

Monkeys don't just eat bananas. They eat leaves, flowers, eggs, seeds, nuts, insects, and even crabs!

Some monkeys work hard for their munchies. Scientists often use monkeys in laboratory experiments. Other monkeys are trained to help people who are paralyzed and need an extra hand. (Some monkeys can even grab things with their tails!) NASA has even sent a monkey into outer space.

That's some serious monkey business!

Did you learn anything? Go back and FILL IN the What Did I Learn? section. Don't forget to CROSS OUT any facts in the first section you got wrong.

Before & After Questions

FILL IN the What Do I Already Know? section.

Topic: China

What Do I Already Know?

_____

_____

_____

_____

_____

_____

_____

What Did I Learn?

_____

_____

_____

_____

_____

_____

_____

_____

_____

Now, READ the article.

Land of the Dragon (and the Panda)

China is the most populous country in the world, with around 1.26 billion people. Compare that to the population of the United States, which is just over 300 million. Don't worry, the Chinese have plenty of room. Their country is the third largest in terms of size, with an area of about six million square miles. That's almost twice as big as the United States!

Did you know that the Chinese people have been using written language longer than anybody else? China is also the source of four important inventions: paper, gunpowder, the compass, and printing.

The Chinese dragon is the national symbol because it stands for power in ancient folklore and art. This long dragon usually has the head of a horse or a lion, with horns. The dragon's body is like a snake's, and it sometimes has little bat wings. The Chinese dragon always has sharp, terrifying teeth and may breathe fire through its mouth and nose.

You can see Chinese dragons marching down the street during celebrations of the lunar New Year (in late January or February). They also fly through the air as kites and ride on the water during dragon boat races.

TURN the page to keep reading!

Now FINISH reading the article.

The most famous real-life Chinese animal is the giant panda. Today wild panda bears mostly live in the mountains of central China. Over time, the panda has become just as much a symbol of China as the traditional dragon. Since pandas are vegetarians (they mostly eat bamboo), they make a much more peaceful symbol than a fire-breathing monster!

Can you believe there are about 40,000 Chinese restaurants in the United States? That's more than McDonald's, Burger Kings, and KFCs combined! But if you think that fortune cookies are traditional Chinese food, think again! Dishes like chow mein and General Tso's chicken are rarely (if ever) eaten in China. However, it is true that most Chinese people eat food with chopsticks, especially when they're eating out of a bowl.

A big country like China has hundreds of stories and fascinating facts. To learn more, try reading a book about it. (Don't forget to check the table of contents first.)

Did you learn anything? Go back and FILL IN the What Did I Learn? section.

 ## Check It!

Cut out the Check It! section on page 9, and see if you got the answers right.

Prepare Yourself

PICK a new nonfiction book to read. Then, READ the table of contents and FILL OUT this worksheet.

The title is _____.

The topic is _____

_____.

Based on the table of contents, I think the book will answer these questions.

1. _____

2. _____

3. _____

4. _____

5. _____

6. _____

When you're done reading, CHECK all the questions that were answered. CROSS OUT the questions that weren't answered.

What other questions did it answer?

1. _____

2. _____

3. _____

4. _____

5. _____

Prepare Yourself

PICK a new nonfiction book to read. Then, READ the table of contents and FILL OUT this worksheet.

The title is _____.

The topic is _____

_____.

Based on the table of contents, I think the book will answer these questions.

1. _____

2. _____

3. _____

4. _____

5. _____

6. _____

When you're done reading, CHECK all the questions that were answered. CROSS OUT the questions that weren't answered.

What other questions did it answer?

1. _____

2. _____

3. _____

4. _____

5. _____

What Do You Know?

PICK a new nonfiction book or article to read today. Before you start reading, FILL OUT this worksheet.

The title is _____.

Before you begin to read:

1. LOOK at the book cover or front page of the article.

2. SKIM through the story.

3. ASK yourself what you know about the subject.

What do I know?

1. _____
2. _____
3. _____
4. _____
5. _____

What did I learn?

1. _____
2. _____
3. _____
4. _____
5. _____

What Do You Know?

PICK a new nonfiction book or article to read today. Before you start, FILL OUT this worksheet.

The title is _____ .

Before you begin to read:

1. LOOK at the book cover or front page of the article.

2. SKIM through the story.

3. ASK yourself what you know about the subject.

What do I know?

1. _____

2. _____

3. _____

4. _____

5. _____

What did I learn?

1. _____

2. _____

3. _____

4. _____

5. _____

Fiction authors can be sneaky about giving you information. You may have to read between the lines to get the whole story!

READ this story.

On the Road

Rachel and Lauren bounced in their seat as they traveled down the bumpy road. In front of them, the rows were filled with kids of all ages, shouting and joking. At each stop, a few would get out. This was the best time of the week. One more stop, then Rachel and Lauren would be free for two whole days!

Now, FILL IN the blanks by reading between the lines.

1. Where are Lauren and Rachel?

    _____

    How do you know?

    _____

2. What day of the week is it?

    _____

    How do you know?

    _____

See? A good story doesn't need to spell out every detail—it lets the reader fill in the blanks. Let's do some more!

Blank Out!

READ this story.

Overheard on Hammond Street

"Hello?" hollered Calvin. "Are you there? I lost you for a second. … Okay, that's better. What? … I'm on Hammond Street, walking to— … No, I won't be home for dinner. Dad said it was okay. Yes! I asked him yesterday. … C'mon! You always do that! Dad says yes, then you say no! Aren't you guys married? You'd think you— … Well, he didn't tell me that. What time is Grandma coming? … Okay, okay, I'm coming home now. What? … All right, I'll stop on my way. A gallon of skim, right? … Got it. Goodbye!"

Now, FILL IN the blanks by reading between the lines.

1. What is Calvin doing as he walks down the street?

   _____

   How do you know?

   _____

2. Who is he talking to?

   _____

   How do you know?

   _____

3. What is he picking up on his way home?

   _____

   How do you know?

   _____

Blank Out!

READ this story.

Busy Builders

Barney would do anything for his family. He and Hilda had built their house together, tearing down the trees, putting them in place, then filling the cracks so that it was warm and snug. The cozy home was just right for their little clan. Marvin, the oldest, was already helping his dad around the dam. He couldn't gnaw down a whole tree yet, but he could help drag the logs and sticks, and pat mud onto them with his flat tail. The youngest, Gretel, helped her mother find fish in the stream. Occasionally they had trouble with their neighbors, a family of humans who didn't like the way Barney had blocked up the stream. So Barney and Hilda would take their family and move to another spot for a while before coming back to build a new house on the stream. It was the perfect place to raise a family!

Now, FILL IN the blanks by reading between the lines.

1. Are Barney and his family humans or animals?

_____

How do you know?

_____

2. How is Hilda related to Barney?

_____

How do you know?

_____

3. What does Barney's family eat?

_____

How do you know?

_____

Blank Out!

READ this story.

Disaster!

Esther looked into the mirror, her big hot tears plopping into the sink one by one. When she heard somebody opening the door, she scurried into the last stall and locked herself in.

"Esther? Are you in here?" It was Esther's best friend Sofia.

"Leave me alone!" moaned Esther.

"C'mon! It's not that bad. Hardly anybody noticed, I swear!"

"Are you kidding? I look like a freak."

"Okay, so you overplucked on one side. It looks kind of uneven, that's all."

"If only Mr. Woodhouse had let me keep my sunglasses on. Then nobody could see."

"Well, you can't stay in here all day. Fifth period is starting."

Then Terry walked in.

"Hey!" yelled Sofia. "You're not allowed in here!"

"Esther!" called Terry. "Is that you in there?"

"Eek!" screamed Esther. "Get out! Get out!"

"I didn't mean to laugh," said Terry. "And I still want to go on Friday."

"No WAY!" sobbed Esther.

"But I've already got my tux. And you've got your dress!"

"And we're sharing a limo!" added Sofia. "You can wear your sunglasses."

"Or a little wig over one eye," laughed Terry.

"That's not funny!" shouted Esther. But she came out of the stall and smiled.

Now, FILL IN the blanks by reading between the lines.

1. Where is Esther? _____

   How do you know? _____

   _____

2. What is Esther doing in front of the mirror? _____

   _____

   How do you know? _____

   _____

3. What is Esther upset about? _____

   How do you know? _____

   _____

4. Is Terry a boy or a girl? _____

   How do you know? _____

   _____

5. Where are they all going on Friday night? _____

   How do you know? _____

   _____

6. Do you think Esther will go with Terry? _____

   Why do you think that? _____

   _____

Blank Out!

READ this story.

Barbecue Blues

I hate this kind of thing. I can't believe I let Marcus talk me into it. It's only been fifteen minutes, and I already have about six pounds of sand in my shoes. Plus, my skin burns very easily.

"Yo, Pete!" calls Marcus. "Come on in! The waves are great."

"No thanks," I grumble.

Of course, the worst thing is the food. Hot dogs, hamburgers, ribs—I can't eat any of that stuff! That's animal cruelty! When I asked if there was any tofu or greens, everyone looked at me funny. At least there's corn on the cob. And I think the potato salad is safe.

This is so boring! I hate to get wet, so I can't hang out with Marcus. Sure, I could bump a stupid ball back and forth over a net with some other kids, but why? It's all so pointless!

Wait a minute! Things just got a whole lot better. There's Christianne Kendall. She's got a comic book I need for my collection. This is my chance to make her an offer she can't refuse!

Now, FILL IN the blanks by reading between the lines.

1. What's the narrator's name? _____

   How do you know? _____

   _____

2. What kind of food does the narrator NOT eat? _____

   How do you know? _____

   _____

3. Where does this scene take place? _____

   How do you know? _____

   _____

4. What is Marcus doing? _____

   How do you know? _____

   _____

5. What game are some other kids playing? _____

   How do you know? _____

   _____

6. What do you think the narrator is going to do next?

   _____

   Why do you think that? _____

   _____

Author! Author!

Now it's YOUR turn! WRITE one side of a cell phone conversation between a kid and a soccer coach. (Tell us the kid's side of the conversation.) Here's the trick: you can't use the words *cell phone*, *soccer*, or *coach*. Make sure your reader knows what's up!

HINT: Why is the kid calling the coach? What other words can you use that will let your reader know what they're talking about? What kinds of things do people say when they're talking on cell phones?

✔ Check It!

Cut out the Check It! section on page 21, and see if you got the answers right.

A good book makes you ask questions along the way, like "What will happen next?" A good reader keeps reading to find the answers.

Check, Please!

READ each paragraph, then CHECK the right answers.

Royal Flush

They say King Minos of Crete had one about 2,800 years ago. The ancient Romans had them too. Queen Elizabeth I had a really nice one way back in 1596. But it wasn't until the late 1800s that a plumber named Thomas Crapper made it possible for everyone to have what they needed most.

1. What question does this paragraph want you to ask?

☐ a. Where is Crete?
☐ b. What year did Elizabeth I become queen?
☐ c. What is this thing that King Minos and Elizabeth I had?

Janey's Bad Day

When Janey walked into dance class, everybody stared. They stared as she crossed the room to put down her bag. They stared as she stretched her legs at the barre. And they especially stared when she got into her position on the dance floor.

2. What question does this paragraph want you to ask?

☐ a. Is Janey a good dancer?
☐ b. Why is everyone staring at Janey?
☐ c. Is this a jazz or ballet class?

READ each paragraph, then CHECK the right answers.

Hanging around the Jungle

In the Amazon jungle, there is an animal like no other. This creature spends a lot of time upside down, hanging from a tree branch. Because his diet is mostly leaves, this mammal doesn't have a lot of energy. So when he moves through the trees (which is rarely), he takes it slow. Really slow.

3. What question does this paragraph want you to ask?

☐ a. What is this animal?
☐ b. How does this animal live?
☐ c. Which part of the Amazon are we talking about?

Mysterious Visitor

Mr. Salazar hated working on Saturdays, but he had a lot to do. By lunchtime, he had already typed up three reports. At the sound of the door opening, Mr. Salazar raised his head. When he saw who was there, the blood drained from his face.

"You!" he gasped. "I thought—I thought you were gone."

"Well," said a voice. "I guess I'm back."

4. What question does this paragraph want you to ask?

☐ a. Why is Mr. Salazar so busy?
☐ b. What does Mr. Salazar do for a living?
☐ c. Who is Mr. Salazar's visitor?

Stop & Go Story

READ the article and FILL IN the blanks along the way.

GO

Wave Rider

In the history of Hawaii, surfing is serious stuff. Ancient leaders used the sport as a training exercise to keep themselves in top physical condition. They also used surfing competitions instead of battles to resolve conflict between people. For a long time, this tradition of surfing was known mainly to the people of Hawaii and other Polynesian cultures. Then Duke Kahanamoku came along and changed the world!

STOP

1. WRITE the question this paragraph makes you ask.

   What did Duke Kahanamoku do to change the world?

   UNDERLINE the part of the paragraph that makes you ask that.

GO

Duke first became famous as a fabulous swimmer. When he was 21 years old, he broke two world swimming records during an amateur swim meet in Honolulu Harbor. But he was so fast, the official record keepers wouldn't believe it! Not surprisingly, Duke easily made the Olympic swimming team in 1912. Throughout his Olympic career, Duke won three gold medals and two silver medals in swimming. And that was only the beginning of an amazing career!

STOP

2. WRITE the question.

   _____

   UNDERLINE the part of the paragraph that makes you ask that.

Stop and Ask

Keep reading!

GO When Duke was finished winning medals at the Olympics, he toured the world, giving swimming shows for his fans. He also brought along his surfboard. Duke had been surfing ever since he was a little boy. In 1917, he rode a single wave (caused by an earthquake) for more than a mile! Duke amazed the crowds by riding his 16-foot-long board, sometimes with another person riding behind. Since Duke was handsome and strong, people loved to watch him. His next career move was obvious.

STOP 3. WRITE the question.

_____

UNDERLINE the part of the paragraph that makes you ask that.

GO Duke headed for Hollywood. From 1925 to 1955, he made more than 30 movies. And, more importantly, he spent a lot of time surfing on the shores of Santa Cruz, California. Duke wasn't the first person to surf in California, but he was the most famous. As a matter of fact, in 1925 Duke made headlines with his surfboard—but not the way you'd think!

STOP 4. WRITE the question.

_____

UNDERLINE the part of the paragraph that makes you ask that.

GO One day, Duke and a few other surfers were hanging out on the beach when a boat capsized not far from shore. The surfers hit the waves with their big boards and saved 12 of the passengers. Duke alone saved eight of them! At the same time, Duke gave the surfboard a whole new job.

STOP 5. WRITE the question.

_____

UNDERLINE the part of the paragraph that makes you ask that.

GO

After Duke's big rescue, lifeguards at beaches started using surfboards to rescue swimmers. Helping others was a big theme in Duke's life. In 1932, Duke became sheriff of Honolulu, Hawaii. Following in the footsteps of his father, who was a police officer, Duke served as sheriff for almost 30 years. His job as sheriff was to greet visitors who came to the city. It was a perfect fit. From the Olympics to Hollywood, Duke Kahanamoku had put Hawaii on the map when it was still a remote island. He was truly the "Ambassador of Aloha." And in 1965, Duke was finally given all the recognition he deserved.

STOP

6. WRITE the question.

_____

UNDERLINE the part of the paragraph that makes you ask that.

GO

When he was 75 years old, Duke's name was added to both the Swimming Hall of Fame and the Surfing Hall of Fame. The record keepers who didn't believe in his first world record had apologized long before. As an athlete and an ambassador, Duke Kahanamoku had always been a legend, and now it's official!

Stop & Go Story

READ the story and FILL IN the blanks along the way.

GO

Snoop is on the Case!

Famous kid detective Snoop Rodriguez found a major mystery waiting for him when he got home from school one day. He stopped dead in his tracks when he opened his front door.

"What the—?" He looked around the living room in astonishment. Then he raced through the house. Every room was the same. "I better get to the bottom of this," he said.

STOP

1. WRITE the question this paragraph makes you ask.

_____

GUESS the answer to your question.

_____

GO

Snoop went back to the living room and looked more closely. Everything had been knocked off the low tables onto the floor. His mother's favorite china frog was in pieces. And there were little black marks of mud on the floor, the furniture, even on the low part of the walls.

"Joey!" cried Snoop. "This mess has 'Joey' written all over it."

STOP

2. WRITE the question. _____

GUESS the answer. _____

GO

Snoop ran into his backyard. Joey was there, tied to his doghouse as usual. His tail thumped the ground at the sight of Snoop.

"All tied up, huh, boy?" said Snoop, rubbing Joey's ears. He checked the little dog's paws. "No mud," he said. "I guess you're in the clear. Hmm...."

STOP

3. WRITE the question. _____

GUESS the answer. _____

GO

Snoop went back inside and cleaned up the living room. He left some of the paw prints because they were important clues. While he was finishing up, the doorbell rang. Snoop opened the door and made a sour face.

"What do *you* want?" he asked.

STOP

4. WRITE the question. _____

    GUESS the answer. _____

GO

Missy Peterson didn't wait to be invited in. She swept past Snoop and sat down on the couch.

"I need your help," she said.

"And why should I help you?" asked Snoop. He still stood by the door as if he wanted her to leave.

Missy laughed. "Are you still mad? C'mon Snoopy! It's been three months!"

STOP

5. WRITE the question. _____

    GUESS the answer. _____

GO

"Yeah," said Snoopy. "Three months since you wrecked my bike and got me grounded."

"It was all for a good cause," said Missy. "We found Fuzzball, right? And I owe you big time."

"Great," said Snoop. "So do me a favor and leave. I'm busy."

"I can't leave," said Missy. "Fuzzball is missing again!"

STOP

6. WRITE the question. _____

    GUESS the answer. _____

Keep reading!

GO

"Fuzzball!" cried Snoop. He raced over to the paw prints. "Yes, it could be, but—wait! There are two sets of prints here."

"What are you talking about?" said Missy.

Just then, the door flew open and Tariq Singleton ran in. "Snoop! You've got to help me! She's gone! I've looked everywhere, but she's gone!"

STOP

7. WRITE the question. _____

   GUESS the answer. _____

GO

"Let me guess," said Snoop. Things were getting clearer now. "Miss Kitty has run away, right?"

"Wow," said Tariq. "You really ARE a great detective!"

"I think I know who made the mess in my living room," said Snoop. "But there's one last puzzle I need to solve." He started looking at all the windows very carefully. "A-ha!"

STOP

8. WRITE the question. _____

   GUESS the answer. _____

GO

"This window is open!" said Snoop. "I bet Fuzzball ran in here, and Miss Kitty chased him all over the house. But where are they now?"

"Let's search the house!" yelled Tariq.

The three kids ran from room to room. Finally, in the basement, they found what they were looking for. Fuzzball the ferret was curled up on the washing machine, fast asleep. Miss Kitty was on the dryer, snoring.

"I guess they wore themselves out," said Snoop. "Now help me clean up the rest of the house before my mom gets home!"

Read between the Lines

CHOOSE a story to read, and try to catch when the author is being tricky—telling you stuff without saying it straight out. WRITE DOWN the clues.

Title of story _____

What is the author talking about? _____

_____

_____

_____

_____

What words does the author NOT use? _____

_____

_____

_____

_____

So how did you figure it out? _____

_____

_____

_____

_____

Read between the Lines

CHOOSE a story to read, and try to catch when the author is being tricky—telling you stuff without saying it straight out. WRITE DOWN the clues.

Title of story _____

What is the author talking about? _____

_____

_____

_____

_____

What words does the author NOT use? _____

_____

_____

_____

_____

So how did you figure it out? _____

_____

_____

_____

_____

Stop and Ask

PICK a new story, book, or article to read today. As you read, FILL OUT this worksheet.

First Paragraph

What question does the first paragraph want you to ask? _____

_____

GUESS the answer. _____

_____

_____

Part way through

What question(s) does the book or article want you to ask? _____

_____

GUESS some of the answers. _____

_____

_____

Almost through

What question(s) does the book or article want you to ask? _____

_____

GUESS some of the answers. _____

_____

_____

Stop and Ask

PICK a new story, book, or article to read today. As you read, FILL OUT this worksheet.

First Paragraph

What question does the first paragraph want you to ask? _____

_____

GUESS the answer. _____

_____

_____

Part way through

What question(s) does the book or article want you to ask? _____

_____

GUESS some of the answers. _____

_____

_____

Almost through

What question(s) does the book or article want you to ask? _____

_____

GUESS some of the answers. _____

_____

_____

Books and stories can be packed with information. But don't worry! Nobody expects you to memorize it as you read. It's okay to go back and reread, or to do a quick CROSS CHECK to refresh your memory.

READ this article.

Shake Up Some Ice Cream!

You can't have ice cream without ice, right? Back in the old days before refrigerators and freezers, the only way to get ice was to cut it from frozen ponds or lakes in the winter. So making ice cream was really hard.

Making your own ice cream is pretty easy nowadays, if you have the time and some ice cubes!

Ingredients:
2 tablespoons of sugar
1 cup of half and half
½ teaspoon of vanilla extract
½ cup of kosher or rock salt
One small and one large resealable bag
Your favorite ice cream toppings
Lots of ice cubes!

Mix the half and half, sugar, and vanilla in the smaller resealable bag. Seal it up tight. Put the ice in the bigger bag with the salt. Before you seal it, put the smaller bag inside too. Then seal the big bag and get shaking! Keep the ice moving all around the smaller bag, so that the half and half freezes up. It should take about 5 to 10 minutes.

When the small bag feels like ice cream, take it out, throw in your fave toppings, and eat. Yum!

Now, TURN the page to answer some questions.

✓ Check It!

Pages 41-42

1. From frozen lakes and ponds in the winter
2. 1 cup
3. 2
4. The smaller one holds the ice cream ingredients, and the larger one holds the ice and salt that freezes it.
5. Shake the resealable bags.
6. Add your favorite toppings!

Pages 43-44
Stop & Go Story

1. super-strong metal, super-fast elevators, and super-cool air conditioning
2. both 40 Wall Street and the Chrysler Building
3. because there's not a lot of room to spread out in cities
4. the Empire State Building
5. 1,670 feet tall
6. in Malaysia

Pages 45-46
Stop & Go Story

1. Snoop Rodriguez
2. Book #7
3. Thursday
4. Brooke
5. Cheryl
6. #6 and #8
7. Thursday
8. Cheryl

Pages 47-48
Stop & Go Story

1. about 43 hours
2. 500,000 gallons
3. air leaks
4. flight deck inspection
5. T–9 minutes
6. Kennedy Space Center in Cape Canaveral, Florida
7. Mission Control in Houston, Texas
8. 3 hours

Cross Check

FILL IN the blanks by answering the questions if you can.
DON'T ANSWER if you can't remember (and don't reread yet!).

1. Where did ice come from before we had refrigerators and freezers?

    _____

2. How much half and half do you need to make ice cream?

    _____

3. How many resealable bags do you need?

    _____

4. What do you use the resealable bags for?

    _____

5. What do you have to do to freeze the ice cream?

    _____

6. What's the very last thing you should do before eating?

    _____

How many blanks did you leave empty? _____

Okay, now go back and CROSS CHECK the questions with the article to
FILL IN any missing answers.

Stop & Go Story

READ the article and FILL IN the blanks along the way.

Race for the Sky

In big cities, there's not a lot of room to spread out. But there's plenty of space if you build up—in fact, the sky's the limit!

We wouldn't have skyscrapers without technology. Tall buildings need super-strong metal to support the weight of so many stories. They also need super-fast elevators to get people to the top. And they need super-cool air conditioning to keep everyone from boiling over (it gets hot on the 100th floor!). Today's skyscrapers are really superbuildings!

They just keep getting taller. In 1930, the tallest building in the world was at 40 Wall Street in New York City (927 feet tall). But not for long! Later that year, the Chrysler Building became the tallest building (1,046 feet). But not for long! In 1931, the Empire State Building (1,250 feet) was finished.

The Empire State Building ruled the roost for more than 40 years. Then in 1971, the World Trade Center (1,368 feet) became the tallest building in the world. But not for long! Three years later, the Sears Tower in Chicago (1,454 feet) grabbed the title. It lasted until 1998 when it was overtaken by the Petronas Twin Towers in Malaysia (1,483 feet). And in 2004, Taipei 101 in Taiwan (1,670 feet) became the tallest building in the world. But not for long!

Now, TURN the page and FILL IN the blanks.

Cross Check

FILL IN the blanks by answering the questions if you can.
DON'T ANSWER if you can't remember (and don't reread yet!).

1. What three things make skyscrapers possible?

_____

2. What was the tallest building in 1930? Hint: This is a trick question.

_____

3. Why do we build skyscrapers so high?

_____

4. Which skyscraper was the tallest building for the longest time?

_____

5. How tall is Taipei 101?

_____

6. Where are the Petronas Twin Towers?

_____

How many blanks did you leave empty? _____

Okay, now go back and CROSS CHECK the questions with the article to FILL IN any missing answers.

Finally, FINISH the article!

GO The race to the sky isn't finished yet. The Burj Dubai in the United Arab Emirates is the world's tallest structure at over 2,000 feet tall. And there are other buildings in the works that might go even higher, including a Mile-High Tower in Saudi Arabia!

Stop & Go Story

READ the story and FILL IN the blanks along the way.

The Mystery of the Missing Mystery

"Okay, confess!" hollered Shakeel. "You borrowed #7 without asking!"

"What are you talking about?" asked his twin sister Brooke. "What's #7?"

"Book seven of *Snoop Rodriguez: Kid Detective!* See? It's supposed to be right on my shelf between #6 and #8, but it's not there!"

"Well, I didn't take it, so stop shouting! Where did you see it last?"

Shakeel thought a minute. Since his Snoop Rodriguez books were really popular, he kept track of them carefully, just like a librarian. So he looked at his notes from last week:

Monday: Eli borrowed #2. Indira returned #7.

Tuesday: Cheryl took #6. Robyn returned #8.

Wednesday: Nadine took #1. Ralph took #5.

Thursday: SCOUT HIKE ALL DAY

Friday: Steven took #10. Eli returned #2 and took #3.

Shakeel showed the list to his sister.

"I think it's pretty obvious," Brooke said. "Just look at your shelf, then ask Mom if anyone came by on Thursday while you were away."

Now, TURN the page and FILL IN the blanks.

Cross Check

STOP FILL IN the blanks by answering the questions if you can.
DON'T ANSWER if you can't remember (and don't reread yet!).

1. What's the name of the detective that stars in Shakeel's books?

   _____

2. Which book is missing? _____

3. What day was Shakeel at the scout hike? _____

4. What is Shakeel's sister's name? _____

5. Who borrowed book #6 on Tuesday? _____

6. What two books does Shakeel say are on his shelf? _____

7. When do you think book #6 was returned? _____

8. So who probably has book #7? _____

How many blanks did you leave empty? _____

Okay, now turn back and CROSS CHECK the questions with the article to FILL IN any missing answers.

Finally, FINISH the article!

GO Shakeel took Brooke's advice and asked his mom. She told him his friend Cheryl had come by on Thursday while he was on the scout hike. She had returned book #6 and borrowed book #7.

"I'm sorry!" Mom said. "It totally slipped my mind."

Mystery solved!

Stop & Go Story

READ the article and FILL IN the blanks along the way.

We Have Liftoff!

The big countdown clock at NASA's Kennedy Space Center lights up about 43 hours before the space shuttle takes off. When the space shuttle is in orbit, it's managed by Mission Control in Houston, Texas. But Launch Control is at Kennedy Space Center in Cape Canaveral, Florida, where the big countdown clock stands in a field. There's about a million things to do to get ready! Here's a sampling:

From T–43 hours (that's "launch time minus 43 hours") to T–20 minutes, the shuttle team checks the steering system and engines. They also load the fuel cells and inspect the flight deck, where the crew will sit and fly the shuttle.

Everyone has to get off the launch pad at T–6 hours because the external fuel tank is being filled with 500,000 gallons of propellants—very dangerous stuff!

The crew enters the shuttle at T–3 hours and begins the last-minute system checks. The shuttle hatch is closed and checked for air leaks. Everyone else clears out.

T–9 minutes and counting! This is when the shuttle team decides whether the launch is really "a go." If so, the bridge leading to the shuttle is retracted (T–7), the shuttle powers up (T–5), there's a final engine test (T–3), the crew members lock their visors (T–2), the sound mufflers are turned on (T–16 seconds), and the main engine is lit (T–6.6 seconds).

T–0 seconds—the rocket booster ignites. We have liftoff!

FILL IN the blanks by answering the questions if you can.
DON'T ANSWER if you can't remember (and don't reread yet!).

1. At how many hours before liftoff does the countdown clock start?

_____

2. How many gallons of propellants does the shuttle fuel tank need?

_____

3. When you check the shuttle hatch, what are you looking for?

_____

4. Which happens first, flight deck inspection or final engine test?

_____

5. When does the team decide whether the launch is a go?

_____

6. Where is Launch Control located?

_____

7. Who manages the shuttle while it's in orbit?

_____

8. How much time does the crew spend in the shuttle before liftoff?

_____

How many blanks did you leave empty? _____

Okay, now go back and CROSS CHECK the questions with the article to FILL IN any missing answers.

Finally, FINISH the article!

GO

About two weeks and 5.7 million miles later, the space shuttle lands again at Kennedy Space Center. If the weather isn't right in Florida, there's a backup landing field for the shuttle at Edwards Air Force Base in California. When it lands there, how does the shuttle get back to Florida for its next mission? It flies piggyback on top of a special airplane! Pretty cool, huh?

You can learn lots of new words as you read. When you stumble on a word you don't know, use the words around it to figure out what it means. Let's see how this works.

READ this paragraph.

> Last winter, my brother and I were sledding down Loggers Hill when I crashed into a tree. I got a cut on my arm that was so big it needed seventeen stitches! Even a year later, there's a long, snaky scar on my arm where the cut was. It's really impressive—I show it to all the kids. Most of them think it's really cool, except for the girls, who think it's gross!

So do you know what *scar* means?

1. Is *scar* a noun (object), a verb (action), or an adjective

   (description)? _____

2. Where is this kid's scar? _____

3. What happened to this kid's arm? _____

4. What is a scar? _____

See, you figured it out. And now you know a new word. Keep going!

✓ Check It!

Page 49

1. noun
2. on his arm
3. He got a big cut on it.
4. It's a mark left behind by a wound.

Page 50

What's the Word?

1. adjective
2. She laughed as if she didn't care.
3. She apologized and helped clean up.
4. She cried because she was sorry she broke the bowl.
5. sorry

Page 51

What's the Word?

1. noun
2. He was on the porch.
3. He was inside the house.
4. He crossed it.
5. doorway or entrance

Page 52

What's the Word?

1. verb
2. down the street
3. on foot
4. He's really proud and vain.
5. to walk as if you're the best thing ever

What's the Word?

Before you read the paragraph, answer this question:

What do you think the word *contrite* means? (It's okay to guess!)

_____

Now READ this paragraph and see if you change your mind.

> I was babysitting for three-year-old Grace when she broke her mom's favorite china bowl. At first, Grace laughed as if she didn't care at all. Then she saw how upset I was and she became contrite. She said she was sorry and helped me clean up. She even cried a little! Then I helped her write an apology for her mom. Grace is a good kid!

1. Is *contrite* being used as a noun, adjective, or verb?

   _____

2. How did Grace act when she first broke the bowl?

   _____

3. What did Grace do when she was *contrite*?

   _____

4. Why did Grace cry?

   _____

5. Now, what do you think the word *contrite* means?

   _____

What's the Word?

What do you think the word *threshold* means? (It's okay to guess!)

_____

Now READ this paragraph and see if you change your mind.

> The soldier stood on the porch, waiting for word from his commander. Mama loomed on the other side of the open doorway, blocking his way into the house. He looked as nervous as I was. Finally his walkie-talkie beeped, and he got his instructions. "I'll have to search the place, ma'am," he said politely.
>
> At that, Mama stepped back, allowing the soldier to cross the threshold into our home.

1. Is *threshold* being used as a noun, adjective, or verb?

_____

2. Where was the soldier at the beginning of the story?

_____

3. Where was the soldier at the end of the story?

_____

4. What did the soldier do with the *threshold*?

_____

5. Now, what do you think the word *threshold* means?

_____

What's the Word?

What do you think the word *swagger* means? (It's okay to guess!)

_____

Now READ this paragraph and see if you change your mind.

> I can't stand Eddie Ross! Everything about him makes me mad. Look at that leather jacket! Does he think he's some kind of tough guy? And he always calls me "babe." Grrr! I especially hate the way he swaggers down the street, with his thumbs in the pockets of his jeans, swinging his hips like he owns the entire planet. Ew! He just *winked* at me. I guess he thinks he's hot or something. As if!

1. Is *swagger* being used as a noun, adjective, or verb?

   _____

2. Where does Eddie *swagger*?

   _____

3. Does Eddie *swagger* in a car or on foot?

   _____

4. What kind of guy is Eddie?

   _____

5. Now, what do you think the word *swagger* means?

   _____

   _____

What's the Word?

What do you think the word *amateur* means? (It's okay to guess!)

_____

Now READ this paragraph and see if you change your mind.

> When the modern Olympic Games began, professional athletes were not allowed to compete. The Games were supposed to feature amateurs who played for love of the sport, not money. In 1912, one athlete was kicked out of the Games because he had once been paid to play baseball. But in the 1970s, the rules against professionals were dropped. When the United States decided to use highly paid NBA basketball stars instead of amateurs, they called them "The Dream Team." Gold medal? No problem!

1. Is *amateur* being used as a noun, adjective, or verb?

_____

2. Is an *amateur* a person, a place, or a thing?

_____

3. In this paragraph, what is the opposite of *amateur*?

_____

4. How is an *amateur* different from its opposite?

_____

5. Now, what do you think the word *amateur* means?

_____

What's the Word?

What do you think the word *abrupt* means? (It's okay to guess!)

_____

Now READ this paragraph and see if you change your mind.

> When Herbie first walked into the bank, the lady behind the desk was kind of rude. She acted like he was wasting her time. After all, what business would a kid like Herbie have at a fancy bank? But when he pulled out the big wad of money he had been saving, the lady had an abrupt change in personality. The second she saw that stack of bills, she got all nicey-nice. She even called Herbie "sir"!

1. Is *abrupt* being used as a noun, adjective, or verb?

   _____

2. What does the word *abrupt* describe?

   _____

3. What happened when the lady saw Herbie's money?

   _____

4. How long did it take for the lady to change her manner toward Herbie?

   _____

5. Now, what do you think the word *abrupt* means?

   _____

What's the Word?

Let's do two words this time!

What do you think the word *descend* means? (It's okay to guess!)

_____

What do you think the word *debris* means? (It's still okay to guess!)

_____

Now READ this paragraph and see if you change your mind.

> To see the wreckage of the *Titanic*, you need a boat to take you 370 miles off the shore of Newfoundland, Canada. You'll also need a submarine to get you to the bottom of the ocean. That's about two miles down! After you descend from the surface to the bottom, the first thing you will see is the front of the ship, almost whole. The *Titanic* broke into two parts as it sank. On the ocean floor, between the two halves, is a wide area of debris from the ship. From the window of your submarine, you may see pieces of metal, broken dishes, jewelry, even some silver coins. But you can't take anything—the site is a memorial to the 1,517 people who died in the wreck.

1. Is *descend* being used as a noun, adjective, or verb? _____

2. When you *descend*, do you move or stay still? _____

3. Where do you *descend* from? _____

4. Where do you *descend* to? _____

5. So what direction do you go when you *descend*? _____

6. Now, what do you think the word *descend* means?

_____

TURN the page to work on *debris*.

FILL IN the blanks to figure out the word.

Tip: Some words aren't pronounced the way you'd think. In *debris* you don't pronounce the "s" at the end (duh-BREE).

7. Is *debris* being used as a noun, adjective, or verb?

_____

8. Where did the *debris* come from?

_____

9. What objects are considered *debris*?

_____

10. Why are those objects considered *debris* now?

_____

11. Now, what do you think the word *debris* means?

_____

Cross Check

PICK a new story, book, or article to read today. As you read, FILL OUT this worksheet.

First page or chapter

WRITE all the details you can remember from the first page or chapter:

_____

_____

Now, CROSS CHECK and add some more. _____

_____

Halfway through

WRITE all the details you can remember from the first half:

_____

_____

Now, CROSS CHECK and add some more. _____

_____

Finished!

WRITE all the details you can remember from the last half:

_____

_____

Now, CROSS CHECK and add some more. _____

_____

Cross Check

PICK a new story, book, or article to read today. As you read, FILL OUT this worksheet.

First page or chapter

WRITE all the details you can remember from the first page or chapter:

_____

_____

Now, CROSS CHECK and add some more. _____

_____

Halfway through

WRITE all the details you can remember from the first half:

_____

_____

Now, CROSS CHECK and add some more. _____

_____

Finished!

WRITE all the details you can remember from the last half:

_____

_____

Now, CROSS CHECK and add some more. _____

_____

Learn New Words

PICK a new story, book, or article to read today. When you see a word you don't know, FILL OUT this worksheet.

The word is _____

The word is used as a   NOUN   VERB   ADJECTIVE   ADVERB
(circle one)

From the context, I think the word means: _____

_____

_____

Now, LOOK UP the word in the dictionary. WRITE DOWN the definition.

_____

_____

_____

_____

_____

_____

Learn New Words

PICK a new story, book, or article to read today. When you see a word you don't know, FILL OUT this worksheet.

The word is _____

The word is used as a   NOUN   VERB   ADJECTIVE   ADVERB
(circle one)

From the context, I think the word means: _____

_____

_____

Now, LOOK UP the word in the dictionary. WRITE DOWN the definition.

_____

_____

_____

_____

_____

_____

Everyone has a right to his or her opinion. But to make an ARGUMENT, you need to back up your opinion with some facts. Can you tell the difference between an opinion and an argument?

READ each statement. CIRCLE A for *argument*, F for *fact*, and O for *opinion*.

1. Blue is the prettiest color in the whole world. A F O

2. Tiffany is taller than Hamid. A F O

3. Kids should vote because they're affected by laws too. A F O

4. Cable TV should be free because I love it! A F O

5. If a kid is old enough to babysit, he doesn't need a sitter. A F O

6. Going for a swim might cool you off. A F O

7. Of course fairies are real! A F O

WRITE an example of a fact.

_____

WRITE an example of an opinion.

_____

WRITE an example of an argument.

_____

When you read an argument, you should see how many FACTS support the OPINION.

Check It!

Page 61

1. O
2. F
3. A
4. O
5. A
6. F
7. O

Suggestions:
Fact: The earth is round.
Opinion: Reggae music is cooler than rock.
Argument: Flying is safer than driving because there are way more car accidents than plane crashes.

Pages 62-63

Suggestions:
YES! Biggie Burger should open.
Facts:
1. The restaurant serves low-priced food.
2. Teenagers can get jobs there.
3. It will bring tax money to the town.
4. People coming to Biggie Burger might shop nearby.

NO! Biggie Burger should not open.
Facts:
1. Fast food is high in salt, fat, and sugar.
2. It might bring strangers to the area.
3. It might take business away from local restaurants.

Pages 64-65

Suggestions:
Quit soccer:
1. more time for homework
2. try a new activity
3. more time for extra chores
4. could make new friends

Stay on team:
1. really good at soccer
2. might be captain next year
3. on the team for two years
4. loves soccer
5. has lots of soccer buds

 **Check It!**

Pages 66-68

Suggestions:
Celebrities make good role models:
1. They bring attention to issues that kids might normally ignore.
2. They show how kids can be just as talented as grownups.
3. Kids can aspire to be as successful as a celebrity.
4. Celebrity bad behavior can be a model for how NOT to be.
5. Some celebrities are well-behaved and good role models.

Celebrities make bad role models:
1. Many celebrities are famous for bad reasons (looks, being rich, etc.).
2. Celebrities sometimes model bad behavior.
3. Celebrities promote products that normal kids can't afford.
4. Many female celebrities starve themselves or get plastic surgery.

Q: Should Biggie Burger open?

First, READ the news story.

Protest at the New Biggie Burger

A crowd of kids and parents held signs and shouted outside the soon-to-be-opened Biggie Burger on Route 73. They were protesting because they don't want the new fast food restaurant to open. Ever.

"This kind of food is really bad for you!" said 12-year-old Diana Wong. "It's high in salt, fat, and sugar."

"Places like this bring strangers to the area," said Diana's mom. "And they take business away from our local restaurants."

Other locals disagree. The mayor insists that Biggie Burger will bring in much-needed tax dollars to help improve the town. And 17-year-old Sandi Corona can't wait for Biggie to open. "I love their fries! Plus, I can get a job there."

Sandi's dad, a construction worker, agrees, "Biggie's prices are just right for a family like ours."

As for Cyrus Matthews, who owns the guitar shop next door to Biggie Burger, he's excited too. "Maybe people who come for a Biggie Burger will swing by and check out my store."

The town will host a meeting on Thursday to hear both sides. Come by and voice your opinion!

READ each argument and FILL IN the supporting facts from the article.

ARGUMENT: *YES! Biggie Burger should open.*

FACTS

1. The restaurant serves low-priced food. _____

2. _____

3. _____

4. _____

ARGUMENT: *NO! Biggie Burger should not open.*

FACTS

1. Fast food is high in salt, fat, and sugar. _____

2. _____

3. _____

4. _____

Which argument has more facts to back it up?

Circle one: the YESes   the NOs

What do YOU think? Should Biggie Burger open? Circle one: YES   NO

Why or why not? _____

_____

You can agree with an argument, even if it has fewer facts supporting it.

Q: Should Paolo quit his soccer team?

First, READ Paolo's letter.

Dear Dad,

I know you've got lots to do with your army unit, but I'm hoping you can help me out anyway. See, I'm thinking of quitting the soccer team, and I want to know your opinion. Don't freak out!

It's just that my homework this year is crazy, and I need more time to get it done. Plus, since I'm the man of the house while you're gone, I've got a few extra chores.

On the other hand, I've put in two years on the team, and the coach says I'll make captain pretty soon. And, of course, I still LOVE soccer! It's way better than any other sport on Earth.

I'm a really good player (or so they tell me). But maybe I could try something new? I've been thinking about photography, actually. My soccer buds are great. We will be friends to the end, but it would be cool to meet some new kids.

What do you think, Dad?

Can't wait for you to come home!

Paolo

So? What do YOU think? Should Paolo quit the team?

FILL IN your argument and SUPPORT it with facts from Paolo's letter.

ARGUMENT

_____

_____

_____

FACTS

Quit soccer

1. _____
2. _____
3. _____
4. _____
5. _____

Stay on team

1. _____
2. _____
3. _____
4. _____
5. _____

Q: Do celebrities make good role models?

First, READ the news story.

Star Spotlight

Lately it seems that young celebrities are making news more than ever before. But is it always bad news?

Thirteen-year-old Chyna Brewster has a poster of her favorite pop star, Stefanie Cruz, hanging on her wall. "I love her music!" she says. "Her songs are about real life—like my life!"

But Chyna's mom is worried. "That Cruz girl is always in the magazines, drinking and smoking. She's not even 18! I don't want my Chyna following in those footsteps."

Chyna laughs at her mom. "I know some kids who want to be famous like Stefanie one day. But I don't know anybody who wants to live her crazy life!"

Dr. Barney Webber, an expert on teenagers, agrees with Chyna's mom. "A lot of these young stars, like that rich party girl Athens Redroof, are famous for all the wrong reasons. Sometimes they're famous just for dating another famous person! That's nothing for kids to look up to. Especially when some young starlets starve themselves or get surgery just to look good."

Geoff Karzai, a 15-year-old skateboarder, says not all celebrities are the same. "Pro skater Dirk Handy came to town last week to help us raise money for a skate park. And, yeah, Athens Redroof sometimes drives on the wrong side of the road, but her boyfriend Jake Greatly visits our troops overseas. And a lot of kids I know talk about pollution because Jake talks about pollution."

"Besides," he adds, "when these stars act dumb, it just shows us how *not* to act, right?"

But Chyna's mom doesn't buy it. She won't buy their products either. "The stuff that these stars promote is way too expensive!" she says. "Last week, Chyna wanted a $1,000 purse that Lana Lonergan wore in her last movie. I told her she could buy it as soon as she earned as much money as Lana did."

Oswaldo Andrade plans to do just that. He and his band Taxicab are getting ready to play on *Star Hunt*, the reality TV show for young talent. "I don't care how a celebrity behaves offstage," says Oswaldo. "I think young stars prove that kids are just as talented as grownups."

No matter what, Chyna Brewster is going to keep her poster on the wall. But her head is in the right place. "When Stefanie Cruz gets in trouble, it's just something funny for my friends and me to talk about. No big deal!"

Make an Argument

So? What do YOU think? Do celebrities make good role models for kids?

FILL IN your argument and SUPPORT it with facts from the article.

ARGUMENT

_____

_____

_____

FACTS

Celebrities make good role models.

1. _____

2. _____

3. _____

4. _____

5. _____

Celebrities make bad role models.

1. _____

2. _____

3. _____

4. _____

5. _____

When you're reading a nonfiction article or book, you should find out about the author. Why? Because the author's point of view on a topic shapes how he or she writes about it. A good reader keeps that in mind!

READ about this author.

Marvin Maxwell

Ever since he was a little boy, Marvin Maxwell wanted to be a jockey, and he learned how to ride a horse before he rode a bicycle. "There's nothing more exciting than watching horses race to the finish line. I was too tall to be a jockey, so I write about horses every chance I get."

1. CHECK the true statement.

☐ a. Marvin would think YES, it's right to race horses.

☐ b. Marvin would think NO, it's not right to race horses.

READ about this author.

Bettina Berkeley

Aliens have visited Bettina Berkeley her entire life. They've taken her to many galaxies and shown her their wonderful cities. This first-hand experience makes Bettina a major expert on extraterrestrial life. "Some people call me crazy," she says. "But they will soon know I'm right."

2. CHECK the true statement.

☐ a. Bettina would think YES, there's life on other planets.

☐ b. Bettina would think NO, there's no life on other planets.

Pages 74-75

Who Wrote This?

1. C
   The author of story C was very proud of Middletown's athletics program, and Alma works for that program.
2. A
   The author of story A seems envious of Joel's success and acts like it wasn't really deserved. Tito has clearly been second place to Joel for a while.
3. B
   The author of story B is worried about Joel dropping out of school, and Hector is proud of the graduation rate.

Page 76

Suggestions:

1. Samoa would think that kids can stay up all night because she clearly stays up every night doing homework, and she loves coffee.
2. Lisa would say bedtime isn't important as long as kids get a lot of sleep because she loves to sleep.
3. Dr. Gilbert Blythe would say kids should go to bed early because he has a lot of kids but likes quiet time alone at night, and he wrote a book about kids getting lots of sleep.

Q: Should kids sell candy door to door?

First, READ the letter.

> Dear Editor:
>
> I don't know about you, but I am sick and tired of kids ringing my doorbell to sell me candy. They always seem to come right when my favorite TV show is on. So annoying! Sure, it's always for a "good cause," like jazz band or a trip to the aquarium, but why should I care? I think kid candy sellers should be stopped!
>
> Yours truly,
> Reginald Reynolds
> Owner of the Candy Arcade on Main Street

Now, ANSWER the questions.

1. What reason does Reginald give for stopping kid candy sellers?

   _____

2. What's another reason that Reginald might want to stop kid candy sellers?

   _____

Do YOU think kids should sell candy door-to-door?

Circle one: YES   NO

Why do you think that?

_____

When you know an author's point of view, it helps you make up your OWN mind!

Q: What should Anna do this summer?

First, READ this letter.

> Dear Anna,
>
> As your best friend, I think it's very important that you have a great summer. So I decided to write you this letter and tell you exactly what you should do.
>
> I know that your mom really wants you to take that babysitting gig with the Shahs at their lake house. That would be a major mistake! You hate lakes, and those Shah kids are total brats. Sure, at the end of the summer, you'd have a lot of money in the bank, but you'd be miserable!
>
> Clearly you should spend the summer lifeguarding at the pool here in town. It's not as much money, but we would have so much fun! Every afternoon we could work on our tans and watch Kareem Singleton do his laps! There's not a lot going on here, but we'd have each other.
>
> Summer only comes once a year. You don't want to mess it up.
>
> XOXO,
> *Magda*
>
> P.S. No need to thank me for this advice. That's what friends are for!

Now, ANSWER the questions.

1. From her letter, do you think Magda is leaving town this summer?

   Circle one: YES   NO

2. What do you think she wants Anna to do this summer? Why?

   _____

   _____

If you were Anna, would YOU stay in town?   Circle one: YES   NO   Why?

   _____

Who Wrote This?

Can you match the story with the author? First, READ these stories.

A. Calling All Klub Kidz!

An exciting new business is coming to Littleboro. Klub Kidz! It's a place where kids ages 12 to 18 can mix and mingle to the beat of some great tunes. Unlike a grownup club, Klub Kidz will only serve soda, juice, and smoothies. And nobody over 18 is allowed on the dance floor!

The best part about the club is the music. The town's best young DJs will spin from 6 p.m. to 9 p.m. every night. The sound system is amazing: two turntables connected to speakers that surround the entire space. The club will play ska, hiphop, and other groovy sounds. Come on out and dance!

B. Korny Klub Kidz

In its latest attempt to be the corniest town on the planet, Littleboro will be opening a club for kids next week. And get this: it's called "Klub Kidz." Cute, huh? The club is painted with bright colors like a preschool, and there's a parent's lounge right next to the dance floor. The menu includes typical kid stuff: milk and cookies, peanut butter and jelly, etc. While it's aimed at kids ages 12 to 18, it's doubtful that anyone over the age of 14 would be caught dead there.

C. Finally, a Place for Local Music!

Attention all rock bands! If you're under 18, you'll finally have a chance to play some gigs. There's a new club coming to town called Klub Kidz. It's for kids ages 12 to 18. There's a dance floor and stage with a great sound system—perfect for live music! The club will feature two new bands every week, so start learning new songs!

Now, READ about these authors.

Nathan Gwirtz has been a regular teen critic for the *Littleboro Gazette* for three years. In the fall, he'll be attending Bigboro University as a freshman. He can't wait to leave small-town life behind.

1. Which Klub Kidz story do you think Nathan wrote?   Circle one: A   B   C

Why do you think that? _____

_____

"DJ Smooooth" (real name Ben Waldman) has been spinning records for parties all over Littleboro since he was ten years old. He was recently voted the best DJ at Littleboro Middle School, and he will be spinning tunes on opening night at Klub Kidz.

2. Which Klub Kidz story do you think DJ Smooooth wrote?   Circle one: A   B   C

Why do you think that? _____

_____

Derrick Zakaria, owner of Klub Kidz, has been promoting new clubs and bands in Littleboro for ten years. He hopes that his new club will attract all the best new talent, as well as kids that love to dance.

3. Which Klub Kidz story do you think Derrick wrote?   Circle one: A   B   C

Why do you think that? _____

_____

Who Wrote This?

Can you match the story with the author? First, READ these stories.

A. Going Pro at 16

It's every kid's dream: a career in professional sports. And now our own Joel Manheim will be living the dream. At only 16 years old, Manheim is joining one of the best basketball teams on the planet. Talk about being in the right place at the right time! The big-shot scouts happened to come to Joel's best game of the season. And, of course, a lot of his success has to do with knowing the right people. Still, we wish him the best of luck!

B. Free-Throwing Your Life Away

While most 16-year-olds will be sitting in class, Middletown resident Joel Manheim will be throwing a ball through a hoop. And earning millions of dollars!

But what if his NBA career falls through? Will he be just another high school dropout? Before he made it big, Joel was an A student, and class president. He would have been welcome at any college! One can only hope that his decision to leave the classroom behind won't harm him in years to come.

C. Chance of a Lifetime!

Everybody's talking about Joel Manheim. And why not? Joel is the product of Middletown's amazing athletic program. He's been playing ball in our gyms and on our fields since he was three years old. He lists three Middletown coaches as his main keys to success. We should be proud of our hometown hero!

Now, READ about these authors.

Alma Sakran, also known as "Coach," has been running Middletown's community athletics for 25 years. She's done it all: little league, soccer, basketball, and track. Her favorite part of her job is working with the kids and watching them grow.

1. Which Joel Manheim story do you think Alma wrote?   Circle one: A   B   C

   Why do you think that? _____

   _____

Tito Molinos, the new captain of Middletown High's basketball team, is the second highest scorer after Joel Manheim. He will probably be team MVP now that Joel has left to go pro.

2. Which Joel Manheim story do you think Tito wrote?   Circle one: A   B   C

   Why do you think that? _____

   _____

Hector Burgess has worked at Middletown High School as an English teacher for 20 years. He's proud to say that while he's been at the school, the percent of students to graduate has increased. Hector is also the advisor to the student council.

3. Which Joel Manheim story do you think Hector wrote?   Circle one: A   B   C

   Why do you think that? _____

   _____

Point of View

Q: What time should kids go to bed?
READ about these authors and ANSWER the questions.

At twelve years old, **Samoa Klein** is the youngest student at Biggieburg University Law School. Her favorite possession is her coffee maker. She has at least eight hours of classes per day and does ten hours of homework each night. Her goal is to become a Supreme Court Justice by the time she's 30.

1. What do you think Samoa Klein would say about kids' bedtimes?

_____

Why do you think that? _____

Biggieburg Junior track star **Lisa Hendrickson** is a record-breaking sprinter. Her key to success? "I take lots of naps." Lisa's favorite day of the week is Saturday because she can sleep all day. Her favorite outfit? "That would be my monkey pajamas!"

2. What do you think Lisa Hendrickson would say about kids' bedtimes?

_____

Why do you think that? _____

A small town doctor for thirty years, **Dr. Gilbert Blythe** is also the father of seven children. He enjoys reading and spending quiet time alone at night. He has studied the effect of sleeplessness on children and wrote the book *Children at Rest Are Children at Their Best*.

3. What do you think Dr. Gilbert Blythe would say about kids' bedtimes?

_____

Why do you think that? _____

Make an Argument

PICK an article from a newspaper or magazine. FILL IN your argument. Then SUPPORT it with facts from the article.

ARGUMENT: _____

FACTS

_____

_____

_____

_____

_____

_____

_____

_____

_____

_____

_____

_____

_____

_____

Make an Argument

PICK an article from a newspaper or magazine. FILL IN your argument. Then SUPPORT it with facts from the article.

ARGUMENT: _____

FACTS

_____

_____

_____

_____

_____

_____

_____

_____

_____

_____

_____

_____

_____

_____

Point of View

PICK a new nonfiction story or book to read today. As you read, FILL OUT this worksheet.

Title: _____

Author: _____

What do you know about the author? _____

_____

_____

Make a list of opinions you read in the story or book.

_____

_____

_____

_____

How are the author's opinions shaped by his or her point of view?

_____

_____

_____

_____

Point of View

PICK a new nonfiction story or book to read today. As you read, FILL OUT this worksheet.

Title: _____

Author: _____

What do you know about the author? _____

_____

_____

Make a list of opinions you read in the story or book.

_____

_____

_____

_____

How are the author's opinions shaped by his or her point of view?

_____

_____

_____

_____

How do you make sure all the information you read doesn't just slide out of your brain? You can make a chart, a diagram, or a timeline!

When you have a lot of events in a story or article, use a TIMELINE to put them in order.

Timeline

READ the article, then FILL IN the timeline.

Computers Then and Now

The first computers weren't for everybody. The Z3 was the first "real" computer, built in 1941 for use by the German government. In 1946, the U.S. Army got its ENIAC computer. (ENIAC is short for Electronic Numerical Integrator and Computer.) The ENIAC took up 1,000 square feet—the size of an apartment!

Thankfully *microprocessors* were invented in 1970, which made computers smaller and cheaper, so soon everyone could have one. In 1982, the Commodore 64 came out for $595. It became the best-selling personal computer of all time.

What happened in each of these years?

Year	Event
1941	
1946	
1970	
1982	

✔ **Check It!**

Page 81
Timeline

Year	Event
1941	The first "real" computer was built.
1946	The ENIAC was built for the U.S. Army.
1970	The microprocessor was invented.
1982	The Commodore 64 came out for $595.

Page 82
Timeline

Time	Event
8:00	Mom told Jake she wasn't doing his laundry.
11:00	Jake broke the washing machine.
1:00	Jake dropped his lunch in the food court.
2:00	Stan Metz took Jake's bus pass.
2:30	Jake started walking home.
5:30	Jake got home, and Mom yelled.
8:00	Jake went to bed.

Page 83
Timeline

Day	Event	Winner
1	3-legged	The Rangers race (Cabin 1)
2	tug of war	Bugjuice (Cabin 2)
3	backward canoeing	Bugjuice (Cabin 2)
4	capture the flag	The Shooflies flag (Cabin 3)
5	obstacle course	The Rangers (Cabin 1)
6	water balloon toss	Bugjuice (Cabin 2)

Page 84
Diagram

Raging Rivers: Cannonball, movie theater
Flood Zone: lame Super Soaker, great minigolf, better food
Both: near home, great wave pools, same bumper boats

Page 85
Diagram

2 Wheels: don't need to push off, can do amazing turns, easy to ride, hard to stop, doesn't balance on its own, tiring
4 Wheels: have to push off to get going, jumps are better, guaranteed balance
Both: same length, same protective gear

✓ Check It!

Page 86
Diagram

Sumo: touch floor with one part of body, can use legs, rice-straw mat, wear a *mawashi*, not in the Olympics, no shoes
Greco-Roman: touch floor with three parts, rubber mat, wear a singlet, wear shoes, in the Olympics
Both: must touch the floor to lose, stepping out of bounds is bad, play inside a circle, play on a mat

Page 87
Chart

Animal	Home	Food
Aye-Aye	Madagascar	grubs
Quokka	Australia	grasses
Capybara	South America	grasses

Pages 88-89
Chart

Roller Coaster	Height/ Length	Speed	Duration
Top Thrill Dragster	420'/ 2,800'	120 mph	17 sec
Kingda Ka	456'/ 3,118'	128 mph	28 sec
Steel Dragon 2000	318'/ 8,133'	95 mph	4 min
Tower of Terror	377'/ 1,235'	100 mph	28 sec

1. Kingda Ka
2. Kingda Ka
3. Steel Dragon 2000
4. Steel Dragon 2000

Page 90
Chart

Name	Team	Color
Ariel	Soaker	red
Raja	Drencher	blue
Nora	Drencher	purple
Ben	Drencher	yellow
Jeremy	Soaker	orange
Sofia	Soaker	green

Timeline

READ the story, then FILL IN the timeline.

Jake's Worst Day Ever!

By 1 o'clock, when I dropped my lunch in the food court, I knew this was the worst day ever. And it wasn't even halfway through! This evil day started at 8 a.m., when Mom told me she was "on strike" and wasn't doing my laundry anymore. By 11, I was up to my knees in the soapy water that was bubbling out of the washing machine. I ran away to the mall for some peace (and lunch). At 2 p.m., Stan Metz and his barfy friends were stealing my bus pass. It took me three hours to walk home! And when I got there at 5:30, Mom was on the warpath. She screamed at me for an hour! Needless to say, I went to bed at 8 p.m., without dinner. Maybe tomorrow will be better!

What was happening to Jake at each of these times?

Time	Event
8:00	
11:00	
1:00	
2:00	
2:30	
5:30	
8:00	

Timeline

READ the story, then FILL IN the timeline.

Cabin Combat

Camp Kiki's 5-Day Cabin Combat was a major success! All three teams fought hard to win each day's event. The Shooflies from Cabin Three had a rough time of it. They lost for the first three days, finally capturing a win in the capture the flag game. Too bad that was their only win!

Cabin One's Rangers and Cabin Two's Bugjuice were neck and neck the whole time. The Rangers scored the first win of the games when their team crossed the finish line during the three-legged race. Then Bugjuice took the crown on day two after easily winning the tug of war. They also won the next day, showing their amazing skills at backward canoeing. All eyes turned to the final event: the obstacle course. Would the Rangers be able to tie up the score? They did! The games went into an extra day. The tie-breaker event was the water balloon toss. You could cut the tension with a knife! After tossing for nearly half an hour, the Rangers let it drop—*splash!* Congratulations, Bugjuice!

What happened each day during the 5-Day Cabin Combat?

Day	Event	Winner
1		
2		
3		
4		
5		
6		

Diagram

If you're reading a story that's comparing two or three subjects, use a DIAGRAM to keep it straight!

READ the story, then FILL IN the blanks.

Splish-Splash Clash!

My twin sister Darla and I can't agree on which water park to go to for our birthday. Both Raging Rivers and Flood Zone are close to our town. My sister likes Flood Zone better. How can she be so wrong? I tried to tell her that Raging Rivers has great thrill rides, like the Cannonball, which drops you over fifty feet! And my favorite thing about Raging Rivers is the movie theater. You can sit in the water and watch a fun 3-D movie! Flood Zone doesn't have that.

Flood Zone has lame rides like the Super Soaker, which is for babies. Both parks have great wave pools, and their bumper boats are pretty much the same. But Darla likes minigolf, and Flood Zone has great courses. They also have better food, I'll admit that. But you don't go to water parks to eat!

It's too bad we can't take both parks and mush them into one!

Raging Rivers	Both	Flood Zone

Diagram

READ the article, then FILL IN the blanks.

Street Surfing

For most of its history, the skateboard rolled along on four wheels. But not anymore! Newer models feature only two wheels with a springy middle that allows riders to "surf" along by twisting with their feet and legs. On a traditional four-wheel board, the rider has to keep pushing off from the pavement in order to get some speed. You don't need to keep pushing a two-wheeler!

The two wheels spin around, so you can do amazing turns, but jumps still work better on a four-wheeler. The two-wheel board is easy to ride but hard to stop because it doesn't balance on its own. It also wipes you out! Your muscles will be sore by the end of the block. The newer board is about the same length as a longer four-wheel board, and you'll need the same kind of protective gear.

If you want guaranteed balance, stick with four wheels. But for an easy, smooth ride and tight turns, drop some wheels and catch the wave!

2 Wheels   **Both**   **4 Wheels**

Diagram

READ the article, then FILL IN the blanks.

Wrestling Two Ways

If you've watched the Olympics, you may have seen Greco-Roman wrestling. But have you ever seen sumo wrestling? Sumo is the ancient (and very popular) art of wrestling in Japan.

The goal of both wrestlers is the same: They want to get their opponents to touch the floor or step out of bounds. In sumo, a losing wrestler only has to touch the floor with any single part of his body (except his feet). A Greco-Roman wrestler must touch with three parts of his body in order to lose a match. In both sports, stepping out of bounds is a losing move. Sumo wrestlers can use their legs to trip their opponents. Greco-Roman wrestlers aren't allowed to use their legs.

Both kinds of wrestlers compete inside a circle drawn on a mat. In the case of Greco-Roman wrestling, the mat is made of rubber. Sumo wrestlers compete on a *dohyo*, a mat of rice-straw bales. Greco-Roman wrestlers wear a *singlet*, which is a tight bodysuit designed to keep wrestlers from grabbing hold of each other's outfit. On the other hand, a sumo wrestler's *mawashi* can legally be used to grab and throw a wrestler out of the ring. Greco-Roman wrestlers also wear shoes during a match, while sumo wrestlers compete barefoot.

Sumo isn't an Olympic sport—yet! But keep your eye out for it.

Sumo	Both	Greco-Roman
_____	_____	_____
_____	_____	_____
_____	_____	_____
_____	_____	_____
_____		_____

Chart

If what you're reading has a lot of characteristics or details to follow, try using a CHART to keep things straight!

READ the story, then FILL IN the chart.

Whacky Animals

Have you ever heard of an aye-aye? That's a little, bug-eyed animal that lives in Madagascar. It loves yummy grubs, and it has a long, skinny middle finger that it uses to dig them out of tree trunks. How about the quokka? It's a marsupial from Australia, with a front pouch like a kangaroo. It chomps on grasses and isn't at all afraid of humans. (But don't feed the quokkas!) Okay, try this one: capybara. Sound familiar? It's the largest rodent in the world—imagine a four foot long squirrel (without a tail). Like the quokka, the capybara chows down on grasses. It lives in South America.

FILL IN the chart with the information from the story.

Animal	Home	Food
Aye-Aye		
Quokka		
Capybara		

Isn't the chart easier to read? Keep going!

Chart

READ the article, then FILL IN the chart on the next page.

Roller Coaster Ups & Downs

When you're comparing roller coasters, you should look at how tall they are (their *height*), how long they are (their *length*), and how fast they go. Let's see how some popular steel roller coasters measure up!

Cedar Point, in Ohio, has the most roller coasters. The Top Thrill Dragster is 420 feet high and 2,800 feet long. Kingda Ka, at Six Flags Great Adventure in New Jersey, is 456 feet tall, 3,118 feet long, and it goes up to 128 miles per hour (mph). That's faster than Top Thrill Dragster, which only gets up to 120 mph. The Steel Dragon 2000 in Japan is 318 feet tall, 8,133 feet long, and goes 95 mph. The Tower of Terror in Australia is 377 feet tall, 1,235 feet long, and goes up to 100 mph.

You can also look at how long the ride lasts (*duration*). The longer the better, right? Well, when you're going this fast, you can't expect a long ride. The Top Thrill Dragster lasts 17 seconds. Kingda Ka and Tower of Terror will both thrill you for 28 seconds. Steel Dragon 2000 gives you four minutes of fun.

Which ride is the best? You be the judge!

FILL IN the chart with the information from the article.

Roller Coaster	Height/Length	Speed	Duration

Now, use your chart to answer these questions.

1. Which is the fastest coaster?

_____

2. Which is the tallest coaster?

_____

3. Which is the longest coaster?

_____

4. Which ride lasts the longest?

_____

Did you use the article or the chart to answer these questions? _____

Chart

READ the story, then FILL IN the chart.

HINT: Read carefully to figure out all the clues!

High Noon on Haddock Street

Let the battle begin! One hot Tuesday afternoon, the kids on Haddock Street filled up their balloons and teamed up to fight a water war. The two teams were the Soakers and the Drenchers. Each of the six kids had their own color of balloon. For instance, Ariel (Soaker) used red balloons. Her brother Raja (Drencher) threw blue ones. (Only a member of Drenchers team threw purple balloons.)

The kids played until each one of them got hit. No player hit a member of the same team. Nora got soaked by a Soaker's green balloon. Ben (who threw yellow balloons) was blasted by a red balloon.

The Drenchers team had two boys and one girl. The Soakers had two girls and one boy. Jeremy was a Soaker. He threw orange balloons. Poor Sofia got hit early on. She only used one of her balloons—to hit Nora.

FILL IN the information you got from the story.

Name	Team	Color

Another way to track information in a story is to map it! For a fictional story, your STORY MAP should include the characters, the setting, the problem, and the solution.

Story Map

READ the story, then FILL IN the story map.

Little Red

Once there was this girl whom everyone called "Little Red" because she wore red clothes all the time. One day, Little Red headed out to visit her grandma on the other side of the big city. When she got to her grandma's apartment, Little Red immediately noticed something wasn't right. First of all, her grandma looked a lot hairier than usual. Second of all, her grandma looked a lot toothier than usual. Third of all, her grandma looked a LOT wolfier than usual! Little Red used her cell phone to call the police. They found her grandma tied up in the closet. "Silly wolf!" said Little Red, as they put him in jail. "You can't fool me."

Characters
_____
_____
_____

Problem
_____
_____
_____

Title
_____
_____
_____

Solution
_____
_____
_____

Setting
_____
_____
_____

Check It!

Page 96

Mind Map

Main Idea: Freaky Speed Records
Details:
1. lawn mower race
2. motorized sofa
3. fastest walk on water
4. fastest walk on hands

Pages 97-98

Mind Map

Big Idea: Silly Sports

In the Water:
1. bog snorkeling
2. Octopush

In the Backyard:
1. cheese rolling
2. toe wrestling
3. Zorb

In a Stadium:
1. chessboxing
2. fistball

Pages 99-100

Mind Map

Big Idea: The Arctic

Animals:
1. Arctic hare
2. lemmings
3. musk-ox
4. caribou
5. seals
6. walrus
7. polar bears

Countries:
1. Denmark (Greenland)
2. Canada
3. United States
4. Russia
5. Iceland
6. Norway

People:
1. Inuit
2. Yupik

Story Map

READ the story, then FILL IN the story map.

Stinkerbell

Taj woke up to find a puppy licking his toes. What a great birthday gift! He named his new best friend Stinkerbell.

The little puppy lived up to her name. She made messes in every corner of Taj's house. She ran away every chance she got. She chewed everything that would fit in her mouth.

Taj tried to teach her, but Stinkerbell wouldn't listen.

"She's just an outdoor dog," said Taj's mom.

One day, they drove Stinkerbell to a farm at the edge of town. She jumped out of the car and ran in circles, barking and wagging like crazy.

"I think she'll be happy here," said Taj, wiping a tear from his cheek.

Characters

_____

_____

Problem	**Title**	**Solution**
_____	_____	_____
_____	_____	_____

Setting

_____

_____

Story Map

READ the story, then FILL IN the story map.

Just for Kicks

It was a beautiful summer day at the beach, but Theresa didn't care. She was carrying a secret that felt like a one-ton weight in the middle of her stomach.

Any minute now, she thought, they'll find out and I'll be in trouble. So far, nobody knew. And that was worse! She kicked herself for listening to Sharice.

"It'll be fun," her friend had said. "We'll do it just for kicks."

So here she was, at the beach with her family, miserable. If only she could tell!

Suddenly her mother put an arm around her. "What's wrong, Tee?" she asked. "You look down in the dumps."

Theresa looked up into her mother's eyes. Maybe she COULD tell!

"Mom," she said, "Sharice and I broke a window in the old Lombard house. Just for kicks."

Sure, Mom was mad. Playing in empty houses isn't safe. It also happens to be illegal. Theresa was in big trouble. Even so, Theresa smiled and began to enjoy the sun and the sand. Even getting in trouble felt better than that secret!

Characters
_____
_____

Problem	Title	Solution
_____	_____	_____
_____	_____	_____

Setting
_____
_____

Story Map

READ the story.

Mall Rats

Zeke and Vin were surrounded. Just when they thought they were goners, Luke dangled a rope from the ceiling of the skate store. "Grab it!" he yelled.

They grabbed, of course. As they climbed up, the rats below tried to jump up onto their legs, but the boys kicked them off.

Mall rats. The worst kind there is. And these were zombies, so you couldn't kill them. Luke, Zeke, and Vin had gone to the mall to hang out three days ago. Now they were climbing in the ceiling above the stores and camping in the camping supply shop.

And they were the lucky ones.

Vin had an idea. He was always the man with the plan. But would it work?

The next day, the boys climbed to the food court. Below them, the cinnamon bun place should have been packed on a Saturday. But it was empty. There were lots of buns sitting in the glass case. Vin lowered himself down to the case and opened the doors. He threw all the cinnamon buns out into the middle of the food court.

The rats took the bait. Every single one of them zipped into the food court and started chowing down on the sticky-sweet treats.

"Let's get out of here!" hollered Vin. He and the others raced for the door.

FILL IN the story map.

	Characters	
	_____	
	_____	
Problem	**Title**	**Solution**
_____	_____	_____
_____		_____
	Setting	
	_____	
	_____	

What was your favorite part of the story?

_____

What do you think happened to the boys next?

_____

Mind Map

When you're reading a nonfiction story, use a MIND MAP to keep track of the main ideas and the details.

READ the story, then FILL IN the mind map.

Fast and Freaky

Want to break a speed record? Hop on your lawn mower and let's go! In England, they've been racing lawn mowers since 1973. During the 12-hour race, the farthest anyone's ever gone is 313.6 miles. That's only 26 miles per hour. Let's try the couch next. One couch potato made a motorized sofa that can go 87 mph. Prefer to walk? A Frenchman walked all the way across the Atlantic Ocean on special ski floats. It took two months. Or you could follow in Johann Hurlinger's footsteps—or handsteps. Johann walked 870 miles on his hands! It took 55 days at about 1.58 miles per hour.

Like they say, it's not where you're going, it's how you get there!

Freaky Speed Records

Main Idea

1. _____

2. _____

3. _____

4. _____

Mind Map

READ the story, then FILL IN the mind map on the next page.

Silly Sports

Do football, baseball, and basketball make you yawn? Well, the world is filled with wild and wacky games you can play in the water, your backyard, or a big stadium.

Grab your snorkel and head to the nearest bog. What's a bog? It's a muddy, smelly bit of swamp. Every year, a village in Wales makes a 200-foot trench in a bog, and people swim two laps, breathing through their snorkel tubes. Or if that doesn't suit you, try a game called Octopush. It's like hockey played at the bottom of a swimming pool, with a puck and tiny hockey sticks. Players breathe through snorkels during the game.

If you prefer to play outside, try cheese rolling. Start at the top of the hill with a big, round, hunk of cheese. Drop the cheese, then chase it. If you can catch the cheese before you get to the bottom, you win. Then there's toe wrestling (like thumb wrestling but using toes instead). But the craziest game of all may be Zorb. To play Zorb, simply get inside a giant, clear plastic ball (like a hamster ball). Start rolling!

If you can fill a stadium with crowds of fans, you should try chessboxing. In chessboxing, players alternate between playing chess and punching each other in the face. But if you don't like either chess or boxing, then that's not the sport for you. Try fistball instead! Like in volleyball, fistballers punch a ball back and forth across a net, using their fists instead of palms. Fistball is a really old sport, dating back to 1555, and it's played all over the world!

Now pick a sport and start training!

TURN the page and FILL IN the mind map.

Make a Map

FILL IN the mind map.

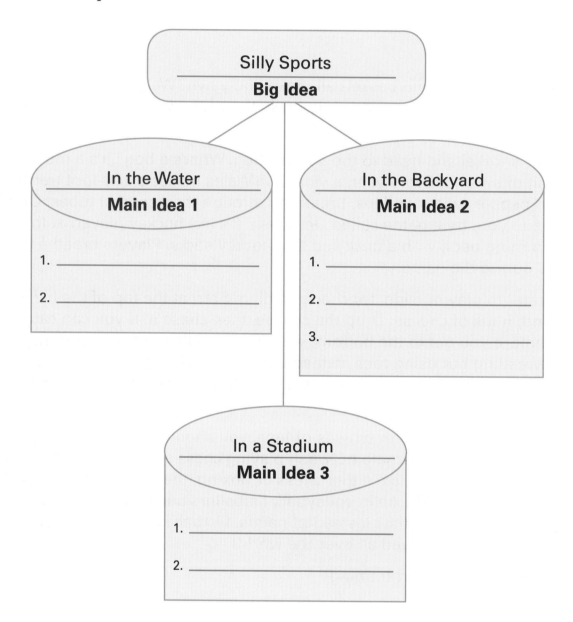

Mind Map

READ the story, then FILL IN the mind map on the next page.

Life at the North Pole

Up at the top of the world, around the North Pole, is an area called The Arctic. Believe it or not, plenty of animals and humans choose to make this region their home, in spite of the cold!

The Arctic's animal residents include the Arctic hare (a kind of rabbit), lemmings (tiny mouse-like creatures), musk-ox (big oxen), and caribou (reindeer). Near the water, you'll find seals, walrus, and polar bears. There are no penguins in the Arctic! They live at the South Pole.

The Arctic includes parts of six different countries. In fact, the entire island of Greenland (which is part of Denmark) is in the Arctic. Parts of Canada, the United States, Russia, Iceland, and Norway are also spread around the North Pole.

The Inuit people live in the Arctic areas of Greenland and Canada. In Alaska and part of Russia, you'll find the Yupik people. Both cultures have lived in the Arctic for many generations, hunting and fishing and raising their families.

It's a rough life. Winters in the Arctic are long, and temperatures can drop to −58°F! But that's balmy compared to the Antarctic. Scientists have measured the Earth's lowest temperature at the South Pole: −129°F! Now *that's* chilly!

TURN the page and FILL IN the mind map.

Make a Map

FILL IN the mind map.

```
                    ┌─────────────────────────┐
                    │       The Arctic        │
                    │        Big Idea         │
                    └─────────────────────────┘
```

Animals
Main Idea 1

1. _____
2. _____
3. _____
4. _____
5. _____
6. _____
7. _____

Countries
Main Idea 2

1. _____
2. _____
3. _____
4. _____
5. _____
6. _____

People
Main Idea 3

1. _____
2. _____

Keep It Straight

PICK an article or story to read, and CHOOSE two subjects to compare. Then FILL OUT this worksheet.

Diagram

The title is _____

I'm comparing

subject 1, _____,

with subject 2, _____.

Details about subject 1

1. _____
2. _____
3. _____
4. _____
5. _____

Details about subject 2

1. _____
2. _____
3. _____
4. _____
5. _____

For each detail, ask yourself if this detail belongs to only one of the subjects or if it is shared by both.

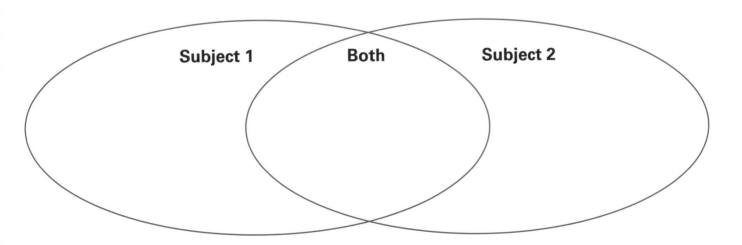

Subject 1 **Both** **Subject 2**

Keep It Straight

PICK a story you've finished reading, then FILL OUT this worksheet.

Chart

Does the story have a lot of characteristics or details? Chart them!

Timeline

Does the story have a lot of events that happen over time? Put them on a timeline!

Time	Event

Make a Map

PICK two stories you've finished reading, then FILL OUT this worksheet.

Story Map

Characters
_____
_____

Problem	**Title**	**Solution**
_____	_____	_____
_____		_____

Setting
_____
_____

Characters
_____
_____

Problem	**Title**	**Solution**
_____	_____	_____
_____		_____

Setting
_____
_____

Make a Map

PICK a nonfiction book or article you've finished reading. Then MAP IT here.

Mind Map

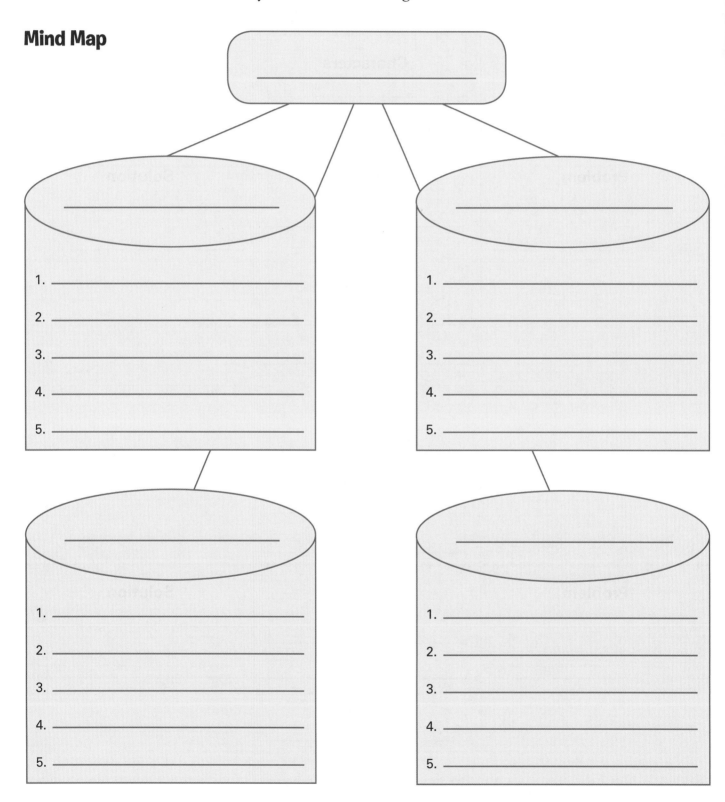

Now it's time to show your skills! Tackle this nonfiction story.

Sneak Peak!

Say you're going to read this book:

First, READ the table of contents.

Now, FILL IN the blanks using information from the table of contents.

1. How much time does this book cover? _____

2. Which chapter might talk about online music stores?

_____

3. Which chapter might talk about radio DJs? _____

4. How long is the longest chapter? _____

Finally, WRITE two more questions that this book might answer.

5. _____

_____

6. _____

_____

✓ Check It!

Page 105

1. 100 years
2. chapter 4
3. chapter 5
4. 11 pages

Suggestions:
5. How did people listen to music before there was electricity?
6. How has the MP3 player affected radio?

Page 106

Suggestions:
Know:
1. Today everyone listens to MP3s.
2. People used to listen to cassette tapes.
3. Radio was invented in the 1920s.
Learned:
1. Before radio and records, people played music themselves.
2. Boom boxes were early portable players.
3. The Walkman tape player came out in the 1980s.

Page 108

Suggestions:
1. How did people finally get music in their cars?
2. Where else did people want to hear music?

Page 109

1. NO
2. Sony Walkman
3. YES
4. **Suggestion:** Author says it revolutionized the music world, thanks Sony, and said they were quick to come out with a CD Walkman.
5. **Suggestion:** The author might work for Sony.
6. argument

Page 110

Good for musicians:
1. Web sites promote new artists.
2. You can download song samples.
3. There are 99 cent songs.
4. People are excited about music.
5. You can hear lots of different music.

Not good for musicians:
1. It's easy to steal songs.
2. There are too many artists.
3. Companies can't promote new artists.
4. The sound quality isn't good.

Check It!

Page 111

1. 1950s
2. There was only live music.
3. CD player
4. player piano
5. radio, record player, reel-to-reel player
6. MPEG-1 Audio Layer 3
7. boom box
8. radio and eight-track
9. over a thousand
10. reel-to-reel players

Page 112

Radio: radio station chooses the playlist, play ads, might hear new music
MP3 Player: you pick the playlist, no ads, no surprises
Both: have playlists, listen through headphones, listen in car

Page 113

Title: Music Players

Decade	Player	Improvement
'20s	Record player	Played recorded music for the first time
'50s	Reel-to-reel	Enabled people to record their own sounds
'60s	Eight-tracks	Built into cars
'70s	Boom boxes	Portable, uses batteries
'80s	Walkman	Easier to carry, uses headphones
'90s	CD players	High quality, fits more songs
2000s	MP3 players	Even more songs, even smaller

1. the '30s and '40s
2. Suggestion: '20s
3. smaller
4. reel-to-reel
5. It's your opinion!

Page 114

Big Idea: 100 Years of Music Players

Music Players:
1. record players
2. radio, reel-to-reel
3. eight-track, boom box
4. Walkman, CD
5. MP3 players

Radio:
1. playlists
2. DJs
3. ads
4. hear new songs

Music on the Internet:
1. bloggers
2. free samples
3. music videos
4. online stores
5. illegal downloads
6. Internet radio

Now, FILL IN the What Do I Already Know? section. After that, you'll be ready to read!

What Do I Already Know?

_____

_____

_____

_____

_____

_____

_____

What Did I Learn?

_____

_____

_____

_____

_____

_____

Stop & Go Story

READ the article and FILL IN the blanks along the way.

Music in the Home

One hundred years ago, there were no MP3s, CDs, or even records! If you wanted to hear a song, you grabbed the sheet music and sang it or played it yourself. Maybe you had a player piano (or a talented family member) that would play a song for you. When a song was very popular, everyone knew how to play it or sing it.

By the 1920s, all of that had changed. Songs could now be delivered to your home in two ways: through a record player or a radio. As people bought record players and radios, they could listen to tons more music since they didn't have to learn to play it first. But radio was usually live, and recording a gramophone record was tricky because the song had to be played perfectly all in one take. And people at home couldn't record their own sounds.

Then a new invention came along that made music much easier to record and play. Magnetic tape allowed different parts of a performance to be cut and spliced together, so that mistakes could be corrected. It also allowed radio and television shows to be recorded, so that they didn't have to air live shows.

So by the 1950s, people had even more music choices. They could listen to music on the radio, on their record players, or on their brand-new reel-to-reel tape player. These early tape players were pretty big, almost like a movie projector. Most importantly, they allowed ordinary people to record their own music (or voice) at home!

CONTINUE READING the story and FILL IN the blanks along the way.

GO

Music on the Go

You can't play a record or reel-to-reel tape while you drive down the street. People wanted to hear their own music in their cars. Sure, the radio had its super-cool DJs spinning the most popular tunes. However, if you wanted to listen to your own music in your car in the 1950s, you were out of luck. But not for long!

STOP 1. WRITE the question this paragraph makes you ask.

_____

GO

In the 1960s, a new product came along: Stereo 8 (usually called "eight-track"). Eight-track tapes were plastic boxes, like big video game cartridges, with a loop of tape inside. Eight-track players were smaller and were built into some cars. Now, while you were driving down the road, you could listen to Elvis or the Beatles. Once people could bring their music along in the car, there was only one place left for it to go.

STOP 2. WRITE the question.

_____

GUESS the answer.

_____

GO

If you wanted to groove down the sidewalk, you had to wait until the 1970s. That's the decade that brought us the cassette tape and the boom box. Boom boxes were pretty big, but they were battery-powered, so you could carry them down the street on your shoulder, blasting your music for everyone to hear. Some boom boxes had special lights on them that would flash to the beat. Right on!

CONTINUE READING the story and FILL IN the blanks along the way.

GO

Sony Makes Music Walk

Finally, the 1980s gave us the Walkman, a small cassette player that came with little headphones so you could bop down the street with your own (private) soundtrack that only you could hear. Sony revolutionized the music world with this one little invention. Thank you, Sony!

The major music breakthrough of the 1990s was the popularity of the compact disc (CD) player. With a tape player, you had to listen to songs in order unless you pressed fast forward or rewind. And tapes used to get tangled! The CD changed all that. The quality of music on a CD was higher than on a tape, and more music could fit on one disc. Of course, Sony was quick to come out with a Walkman for CDs too.

But that isn't the end of the story. Step into the 21st century, and see what happens next!

STOP Stop and think about the author's point of view.

1. Before this page, has the author named any brand or company?

   CIRCLE one: YES   NO

2. What is the brand or company name mentioned here? _____

3. Does this author seem to like this brand or company?

   CIRCLE one: YES   NO

4. How do you know? _____

5. What's one reason why the author might talk about Sony this way?

   _____

6. Is the last sentence of the first paragraph a fact or an argument?

   _____

CONTINUE READING the story and FILL IN the blanks along the way.

The Internet: Good for Musicians?

The Internet has changed so many things, especially music. You can hear lots of different music online. There are bloggers who write about new artists, band sites with free song samples and music videos, plus online stores where you can buy songs for 99 cents.

Of course, most of this is possible because of the MP3. That stands for "MPEG-1 Audio Layer 3," and it's a way of storing data on a computer so that it doesn't take up too much space. An MP3 player can be tiny, even smaller than a Walkman. And it can hold over a thousand songs. It seems like people are more excited about music than ever before!

Some people think the Internet has hurt musicians. There are illegal sites that let you download songs for free, so the artists don't make any money. With so many musicians out there, how can any one band be as big as the Beatles? Big record companies can't make much money on single 99 cent song sales, so they don't promote their new artists. Plus, lots of music lovers complain that the sound of MP3s doesn't have the quality of records or CDs.

So what do YOU think? Is the Internet good for musicians?

FILL IN your argument and SUPPORT it with facts from the story.

ARGUMENT: _____

FACT 1: _____

FACT 2: _____

FACT 3: _____

FACT 4: _____

FACT 5: _____

FILL IN the blanks by answering the questions, if you can. DON'T ANSWER if you can't remember (and don't reread yet!).

1. In what decade did many people start using reel-to-reel players? _____

2. How did people hear songs before records and radios?

   _____

3. What was the popular kind of music player in the 1990s? _____

4. Which invention came first, the player piano or the radio?

   _____

5. What music player options did people have in the 1950s?

   _____

6. What does "MP3" stand for? _____

7. Which player did people carry on their shoulders?_____

8. What two kinds of music players worked in a 1960s car?

   _____

9. About how many songs can an MP3 hold? _____

10. Which player first allowed people to record their own music at home?

   _____

How many blanks did you leave empty? _____

Okay, go back and CROSS CHECK the questions against the article to FILL IN any missing answers.

Now, KEEP READING on the next page.

CONTINUE READING the story and FILL IN the blanks along the way.

GO

Radio or MP3 Player?

Today, radio stations are still playing music up and down the dial, and on the Internet. What's the difference between listening to songs on a radio and listening on your own MP3 player? They both have *playlists*—a list of songs that can be heard. On the radio, someone in a big office may choose that list, then the DJ puts those songs on the air in whatever order she wants. Your MP3 playlist is created by *you*, right? You pick the order or "shuffle" it. Most radio stations also have yappy commercials that play between songs. When you listen to your MP3 player, you don't hear any ads (unless you want to). On the radio, you might hear a song you've never heard before—and you might *love* it (or not). There are no surprises when you listen to your own MP3 playlist. Whether it's radio or MP3, you can listen to music through your headphones or in your car. You can drown out the world with rocking tunes!

STOP

Radio   Both   MP3 Player

_____   _____   _____

_____   _____   _____

_____   _____   _____

FILL IN this combination chart and timeline with information from the story.

Decade	Music Player	Improvement
1920s	Record player	Played recorded music for the first time
1950s		
1960s		
1970s		
1980s		
1990s		
2000s		

Use your chart to answer these questions.

1. What two decades are missing in the progress of home music players?

   _____

2. In your opinion, which decade made the most progress? Why?

   _____

3. Over the years, have music players gotten bigger, or smaller?

   _____

4. Which came first, the Walkman or the reel-to-reel?

   _____

5. Which is more important to you, high-quality sound, or being able to carry your music wherever you go?

   _____

FILL IN this mind map for the story you just read.

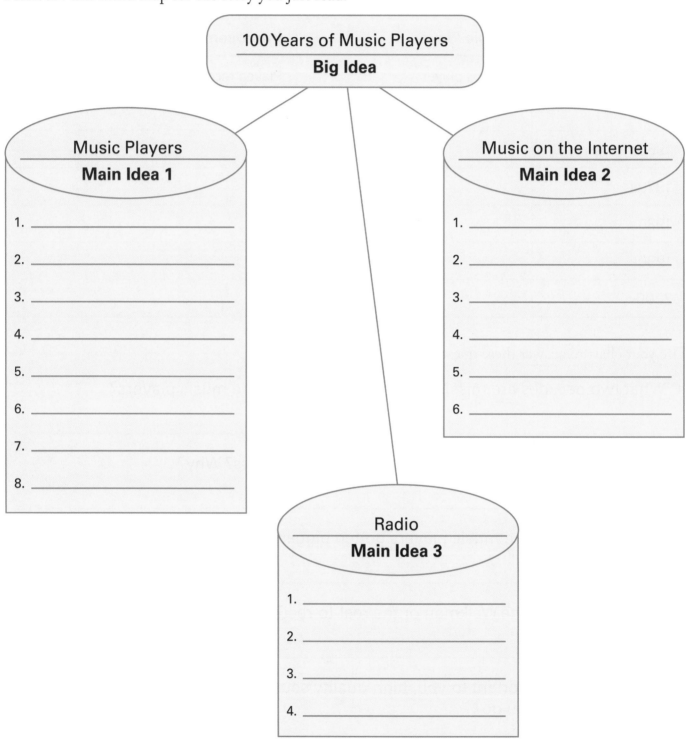

100 Years of Music Players
Big Idea

Music Players
Main Idea 1

1. _____
2. _____
3. _____
4. _____
5. _____
6. _____
7. _____
8. _____

Music on the Internet
Main Idea 2

1. _____
2. _____
3. _____
4. _____
5. _____
6. _____

Radio
Main Idea 3

1. _____
2. _____
3. _____
4. _____

What did you learn from this article? Go back to page 106 and FILL IN the What Did I Learn? section.

Stop & Go Story

Ready to work with some fiction? Go ahead, show off what you know!

READ the story and FILL IN the blanks along the way.

GO

Snoop Solves It!

One Monday morning, Snoop Rodriguez's phone rang. The famous kid detective picked it up and listened. When he heard who it was, he stood up straight and practically saluted.

"Y-y-es sir!" he said. "Of course! Right away, sir!"

Snoop grabbed his skateboard and ran out the door. He arrived at the police station in seven minutes flat.

"Thanks for coming so quickly, Snoop," Chief Sharif said when Snoop walked into his office. "We've got a serious problem."

"You mean First Federal?" asked Snoop.

"That's right, my boy!" The chief was impressed. "I guess you read about it in the newspaper. Biggest bank robbery we've ever had. It happened just two days ago, but the trail's cold as a dog's nose. And that's not all."

"What else?" asked Snoop.

"The Lazlo Gallery was hit last night. The thieves took off with 10 priceless paintings. Both the bank and the gallery were locked up tight. There's no way a person could get in!"

"Hmmm..." Snoop's brain was already on the job.

"Luckily they left this behind." The chief threw something on the table.

Snoop frowned. "Who ate the banana?" he asked.

"That's what we need you to find out."

✓ Check It!

Page 116

1. You know it was Chief Sharif because Snoop practically saluted, then went to see the chief when he arrived at the police station.
2. You know Snoop used his skateboard because he grabbed it and ran out the door, then arrived at the police station.
3. You know First Federal is a bank because Chief said, "Biggest bank robbery we've ever had."
4. You know it happened on Saturday because Chief said on Monday that it happened two days ago.
5. You know the Chief has no clues because he said the trail was cold.
6. You know the thieves left a banana peel because Snoop asked who ate the banana.

Page 117

1. What big thing is happening in Lazlo?
2. Unless what?

Page 118

1. noun
2. She was doing her afternoon show in front of dozens of people.
3. She was alone and couldn't prove she wasn't robbing the gallery.
4. proof that you were somewhere else when a crime was committed

Check It!

Page 120

Day	Event
Sat	First Federal Bank is robbed.
Sun	Lazlo Gallery is robbed.
Mon	Chief Sharif calls in Snoop Rodriguez.
Tue	Snoop talks to The Amazing Krupa.
Wed	Snoop goes to the circus.
Thu	The police arrest Marvin and his trainer.

Title: Snoop Solves It!
Characters: Snoop Rodriguez, The Amazing Krupa, Chief Sharif, Eliza , Marvin the Magnificent, Dirk Andrews the trainer
Setting: Lazlo, a small town
Problem: A crime wave has hit Lazlo.
Solution: Snoop figures out that the crime was done by a monkey and his trainer.

 Now, FILL IN the blanks by reading between the lines.

1. Who called Snoop on Monday morning? _____

   How do you know? _____

   _____

2. How did Snoop get to the police station? _____

   How do you know? _____

   _____

3. What is First Federal? _____

   How do you know? _____

   _____

4. On what day of the week did the bank robbery happen?

   _____

   How do you know? _____

   _____

5. Does the chief have any clues from the bank robbery? _____

   How do you know? _____

6. What is the clue that the thieves left behind at the gallery?

   _____

   How do you know? _____

   _____

CONTINUE READING the story and FILL IN the blanks along the way.

GO

On Tuesday, Snoop rode his bike around town, thinking hard. Two big robberies in one weekend! That was really weird. Things like that didn't happen in a town like Lazlo. Nothing big ever happened here. Suddenly Snoop stopped. That's not totally true, he thought. There is *one* big thing happening.

STOP

1. WRITE the question this paragraph makes you ask.

_____

GUESS the answer. _____

GO

Snoop pedaled like crazy, racing to the center of town. He stopped outside the Lazlo Theater, where a big sign said The Amazing Krupa Magic Show!

As he stared at the sign, Snoop's brain was working overtime. Both the bank and the art gallery had been locked up tight. There was no way anybody could get in. Unless…

STOP

2. WRITE the question.

_____

GUESS the answer. _____

GO

Snoop decided to pay a visit to The Amazing Krupa. He found her practicing her act in the empty theater. She stepped inside a small box and crouched while her assistant placed the lid on top, then nailed it shut. How can she breathe in there? Snoop wondered. Five minutes later, Krupa had escaped from the little box.

"Ms. Krupa," called Snoop, "I'd like to ask you a few questions."

STOP What do you think the word *alibi* means? (It's okay to guess!)

_____

Now CONTINUE reading and see if you change your mind.

GO Snoop told The Amazing Krupa about the robberies. He asked her if she had an alibi for Saturday and Sunday.

"I have an alibi for one day," said The Amazing Krupa. "And it's rock solid. On Saturday, while the bank was being robbed, I was here, doing my afternoon show. Dozens of people saw me. But Sunday night, I don't have an alibi. I was alone in my hotel room. I can't prove that I wasn't robbing the gallery."

STOP 1. Is *alibi* being used as a noun, adjective, or verb? _____

2. What was The Amazing Krupa's *alibi* for Saturday?

_____

3. Why didn't The Amazing Krupa have an *alibi* for Sunday night?

_____

4. Now, what do you think the word *alibi* means?

_____

GO

Snoop thanked The Amazing Krupa and left the theater. I don't think she did it, he thought. That means I'm swimming without fins.

The next day, Snoop's little sister Eliza woke him up. "It's circus day!" she yelled. "You promised to take me again before they leave town."

"I totally forgot!" Snoop smiled. The circus had never come to Lazlo before. Snoop hadn't seen it yet, but Eliza had been there three times already.

The circus was on the edge of town in a big field. Eliza dragged Snoop from the Tilt-a-Whirl, to the cotton candy cart, to the Tent of Wonders. She really knew her way around!

"I'm saving the best for last," Eliza said.

"What's that?" asked Snoop.

"Marvin the Magnificent!" She pulled him into a tent that was decorated with banana trees.

An hour later, Snoop and Eliza left the tent. "Wasn't that the coolest thing you ever saw?" squealed Eliza. "Marvin is such a cute monkey! I love when he picks the lock and steals the bananas out of the safe!"

Snoop nodded. As soon as he got home, he called the chief. "I think I know who our robbers are," he said.

As the circus folk packed up their tents Thursday morning, the Lazlo police pulled into the field. Chief Sharif walked up to the circus owner.

"We're here to arrest Marvin the Magnificent and his trainer Dirk Andrews!"

FILL IN the timeline for the story.

Day	Event
Saturday	
Sunday	
Monday	
Tuesday	
Wednesday	
Thursday	

FILL IN the story map for this story.

Characters

_____

_____

_____

Problem	**Title**	**Solution**
_____		_____
_____	_____	_____
_____		_____

Setting

_____

_____

_____

_____